A Photographic Geography of Alaska

ALASKA GEOGRAPHIC®
Volume 7, Number 2, 1980

The Alaska Geographic Society

To teach many more to better know and use our natural resources

Editors: Robert A. Henning, Barbara Olds, Penny Rennick
Associate Editors: Margy Kotick, Lael Morgan, Carol Phillips
Designer: Dianne Hofbeck
Cartographer: Jon.Hersh
Illustrator: Val Paul Taylor

Editor's note: Population figures for this issue were compiled in 1978-1979 and are courtesy of the State of Alaska, Department of Community and Regional Affairs, Local Government Assistance Division, Juneau, Alaska.

ALASKA GEOGRAPHIC®, ISSN 0361-1353, is published quarterly by The Alaska Geographic Society, Anchorage, Alaska 99509. Second-class postage paid in Edmonds, Washington 98020. Printed in U.S.A.

THE ALASKA GEOGRAPHIC SOCIETY is a nonprofit organization exploring new frontiers of knowledge across the lands of the polar rim, learning how other men and other countries live in their Norths, putting the geography book back in the classroom, exploring new methods of teaching and learning—sharing in the excitement of discovery in man's wonderful new world north of 51°16'.

MEMBERS OF THE SOCIETY RECEIVE *Alaska Geographic*®, a quality magazine in color which devotes each quarterly issue to monographic indepth coverage of a northern geographic region or resource-oriented subject.

MEMBERSHIP DUES in The Alaska Geographic Society are $20 per year; $24 to non-U.S. addresses. (Eighty percent of each year's dues is for a one-year subscription to *Alaska Geographic*®.) Order from The Alaska Geographic Society, Box 4-EEE, Anchorage, Alaska 99509; (907) 274-0521.

MATERIAL SOUGHT: The editors of *Alaska Geographic*® seek a wide variety of informative material on the lands north of 51°16' on geographic subjects—anything to do with resources and their uses (with heavy emphasis on quality color photography)—from Alaska, Northern Canada, Siberia, Japan—all geographic areas that have a relationship to Alaska in a physical or economic sense. In early 1980 editors were seeking material on the following geographic regions and subjects: the Kobuk-Noatak area and glaciers of Alaska. We do not want material done in excessive scientific terminology. A query to the editors is suggested. Payments are made for all material upon publication.

CHANGE OF ADDRESS: The post office does not automatically forward *Alaska Geographic*® when you move. To insure continuous service, notify us six weeks before moving. Send us your new address and zip code (and moving date), your old address and zip code, and if possible send a mailing label from a copy of *Alaska Geographic*®. Send this information to *Alaska Geographic*® Mailing Offices, 130 Second Avenue South, Edmonds, Washington 98020.

MAILING LISTS: We have begun making our members' names and addresses available to carefully screened publications and companies whose products and activities might be of interest to you. If you would prefer not to receive such mailings, please so advise us, and include your mailing label (or your name and address if label is not available).

The cover: The six Alaskas within Alaska.
►Top row from left, Auke Bay near Juneau in Southeast; see chapter beginning on page 8. (The Jerrold Olsons) / Wonder Lake, Mount McKinley National Park in the Interior; see page 54. (Jim Shives) / Columbia Glacier, Prince William Sound, in the Southcentral/Gulf Coast region; see page 30. (Ron Dalby)
►Bottom row from left, polar bear on an ice floe in the Arctic; see page 110. (Steve McCutcheon) / Banding geese on Buldir Island in the Aleutians; see page 74. (R.H. Day) / Leads in the pack ice along the Bering Sea coast; see page 92. (Steve Leatherwood)

Contents page
Russell Glacier on Chitistone Pass separates the Wrangell from the Saint Elias mountains. The shoulder of 16,421-foot Mount Bona is on the left horizon; peaks of the University Range are on center and right horizon.
(George Herben)

Below
Old Rampart, on the right bank of the Porcupine River, was once one of the largest settlements on the river.
(Alan C. Paulson)

Introduction

Alaska is so vast, so thinly populated, and has so many insular villages and cities separated one from the other by great distances that it is difficult to visualize, even for local residents. Most residents know little about most of Alaska . . . and that just about sums up the situation. There is a growing library of published Alaska material, from the seen-by-few Aleutian Islands to the heavily populated Rail Belt, the Anchorage and Fairbanks area, to the disconnected "panhandle" of Southeast Alaska and its glaciers and fjords as well as the bleak but oil-rich Arctic Slope in the opposite direction . . . but unfortunately much of it is either stuffy academic material or rehash of older and also thin research resulting too often in the "quickie" book or article by another two-week visitor. As we've said, the Alaskan resident himself often knows but little about this big country. Even we in The Alaska Geographic Society and Alaska Northwest Publishing, whose business has been digging for Alaska knowledge and publishing for nearly half a century, must admit we are constantly discovering new elements of Alaska, even newly explored physical areas. So don't feel badly if you regret your knowledge of Alaska is limited. So is ours.

Because the job of "doing an Alaska geography" is so big, so complex, we felt this compendium of a lot of wonderful color photos and a digest of "adequate" information . . . facts . . . would serve better to impart an improved understanding of Alaska in all its aspects. We've borrowed heavily from *ALASKA*® magazine, from other issues of *ALASKA GEOGRAPHIC*® and from our *ALASKA ALMANAC*. We hope you enjoy it. In a sense it is our family album.

—The Editors

Separated by the waters of Iliuliuk Harbor, Unalaska (foreground) and Dutch Harbor on adjacent Amaknak Island are one community for business purposes.
(Ben Kirker)

The Six Alaskas

Aleutia

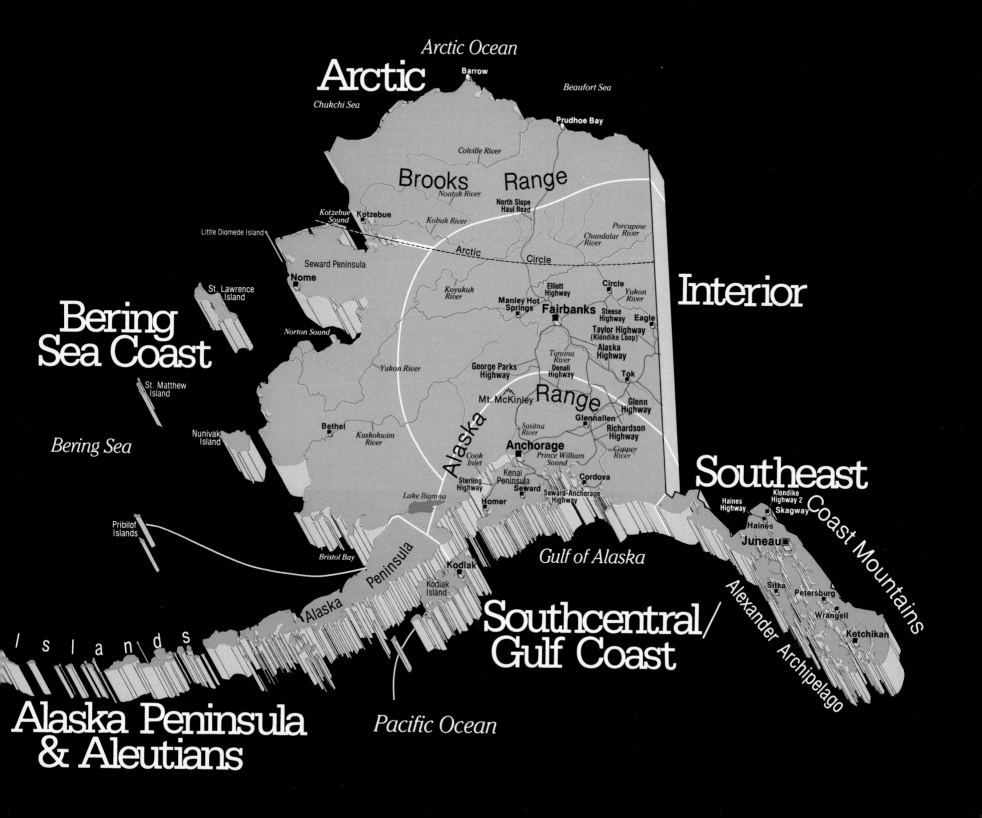

Southeast

Forested islands and glacier-scoured fjords against a mountain backdrop . . . this is Southeast, the panhandle that extends some 560 miles from Dixon Entrance near Ketchikan to Icy Bay north of Yakutat. Geological activity has sculpted more than a thousand islands in Southeast, including Prince of Wales, third largest in the United States at 2,231 square miles. The region's narrow strip of mainland is isolated from the rest of North America by the Saint Elias and Coast mountain ranges. Mount Saint Elias (18,008 feet), Mount Vancouver (15,700 feet), Mount Fairweather (15,300 feet) and other lofty peaks make the Saint Elias the highest coastal range in the world.

Average precipitation in Southeast is more than 100 inches in many spots, ranging from 26 inches at Skagway to 227 inches at Little Port Walter on Baranof Island. Warm ocean currents moderate the region's climate. Summer temperatures average close to 60°F. Sub-zero temperatures are not common in winter and the thermometer usually hovers in the mid-thirties. At lower elevations snows often melt within a few days; higher up, more than 200 inches are recorded each year—snow that continually feeds the 40- by 100-mile Juneau Icefield.

Heavy rainfall and a mild climate encourage timber growth and more than 73% of Southeast is covered with dense forests. Covering 16 million acres, the Tongass National Forest, composed primarily of western hemlock and Sitka spruce interspersed with red cedar and Alaska yellow cedar, is the nation's largest. Ground cover is lush and includes devil's club, blueberries, huckleberries, mosses and ferns.

The heavy timber and dense undergrowth is prime habitat for Sitka blacktail deer, wolves and bears. Brown/grizzlies inhabit Admiralty, Baranof and Chichagof islands (no wolves) and the mainland; black bears inhabit other forested islands and the mainland. Mountain goats, lynx, wolverines, foxes, mink, river otters, porcupines, marten, scattered populations of moose

9

Above
One of the many access routes to Alaska is the Inside Passage, a water route from Seattle, Washington, to Skagway, Alaska. This ferry is passing through Grenville Channel, south of Prince Rupert, British Columbia.
(Sally Bishop)

Opposite
Devils Thumb (9,077 feet) rises on the Alaska-Canada border northeast of Petersburg.
(Michio Hoshino)

and an assortment of small mammals range throughout Southeast. The region boasts the largest bald eagle population in the world.

Three-fourths of Southeast's 59,000 residents live in five major urban areas: Ketchikan, Wrangell, Petersburg, Sitka and Juneau. About 25 smaller communities, some with fewer than 50 inhabitants, are scattered among the islands and mainland. Tlingit, Haida, and Tsimshian Indians live in the major communities and in traditional villages such as Klukwan, Hoonah, Angoon, Kasaan, Kake, Klawock, Hydaburg and Metlakatla.

Access to Southeast Alaska, either from the continental United States or from Central Alaska to the north and west, is by air or via the Alaska Highway, connecting with Alaska state ferries at Haines, over the Haines Highway, Skagway via the newly opened Skagway-Carcross, Yukon Territory, and Whitehorse, Yukon Territory, road, known as the Klondike Highway, or Yellowhead 16 Canadian highway route ending at Prince Rupert, British Columbia. Canadian National Railways goes to Prince Rupert. White Pass & Yukon Route narrow-gauge rail (spectacularly scenic) runs from tidewater at Skagway to Whitehorse on the Yukon River in Yukon Territory.

Ketchikan, with a population of about 14,600, serves as the southern gateway to the region. For many years the huge salmon catches for which Southeast was famous centered around this port. Today the pulp and timber industry, tourism, fishing and the related businesses of fish processing and cold storage support the economy.

Timber forms the basis for the major industry for Ketchikan and most of Southeast. Ketchikan Spruce Mill, now part of Louisiana Pacific, Ketchikan Division, was founded in 1903 and is the longest continuously operated mill in the state. Louisiana Pacific also operates a pulp mill just north of Ketchikan and the Annette Island sawmill. Louisiana Pacific's operations near Ketchikan process between 250 million and 300 million board feet annually. The pulp, a dissolving variety suitable for breads, frostings, pharmaceuticals, photo film, rayon and cellophane, is shipped to domestic and foreign markets. About 15 camps supply logs for Louisiana Pacific's operations in the Ketchikan area.

Several communities near Ketchikan rely on fishing or logging for their livelihood. Metlakatla, in addition to being the site of the Annette Island sawmill, has had a salmon cannery since 1890. Hyder, tucked away at the end of 70-mile-long Portland Canal, is a former mining boom town. A side road off the Cassiar Highway connects Hyder with its neighbor, Stewart, British Columbia, and the rest of the continent. Myers Chuck, north of Ketchikan on the

Cleveland Peninsula, is a small fishing village that was dying a few years ago but has lately seen an increase in activity.

A little over 40 miles directly east of Ketchikan is a deposit estimated to contain a reputed 700 million tons of molybdenum sulfide. U.S. Borax & Chemical Corporation wants to develop the site at Quartz Hill, a knob in the valley between the Wilson and Keta rivers and ship concentrates to U.S. and foreign markets. Since the ore is close to the surface, corporation officials anticipate an open-pit mine. Molybdenum is used as a lubricant for oil and grease and as a steel alloy to increase durability, lighten weight, and provide thermal flexibility to allow steel to perform under extremely high and low temperatures.

Several towns dependent on fishing and/or logging are nestled on Prince of Wales Island. Ferries stop at Hollis on the east side of the island and from there you can travel by road to Craig, Klawock and Thorne Bay. Mining, especially for copper, has always been important to this region, and while none of the mining camps have survived, there is still much prospecting activity in the area.

About 85 miles northwest of Ketchikan is Wrangell, population about 3,000, the only Alaska city to have existed under three flags—Russian, British and American. Its location near the mouth of the Stikine River, offering water passage through the Coast Mountains, enabled Wrangell to take advantage of the mining and commerce on the river. Mainstays of the community's economy today are fishing, including the canning of shrimp, crab and salmon, and freezing of salmon and halibut; and forest products. Two large mills, operated by Alaska Lumber and Pulp, employ about 130 people. The plant in downtown Wrangell processes 250,000 board feet per eight-hour shift. There logs, primarily spruce, are cut; sawdust is converted into fuel to generate electricity to operate the plant; and pulp chips are sent to Sitka for processing. The plant south of town, known as the 6½-Mile Mill,

handles about 30 million board feet annually and concentrates on cutting hemlock into four-by-fours.

Midway between Ketchikan and Juneau is Petersburg, population about 3,000. Spread out along the shores of Mitkof Island, Petersburg thrives on a modern fishing industry. Icicle Seafoods, Inc., one of the state's largest home-owned fisheries enterprises, sold about $60 million worth of fish products in 1978. The plant in Petersburg handles salmon, herring, tanner and king crab, and bottom fish such as pollack, halibut and flounder. Facilities are also available for freezing and converting fish meal into a high-protein additive for animal feed. Whitney-Fidalgo Seafoods, Inc., and Alaska Glacier Seafoods also operate salmon and shrimp canneries in Petersburg. In the midst of all the fish processing is Mitkof Lumber, a small mill that handles local spruce and hemlock.

Sitka, population 7,200, is located on the west coast of Baranof Island at the foot of Harbor Mountain and looks out over an archipelago of islands to the vast North Pacific. Once the capital of Russian America, Sitka is capitalizing on its rich historical past and scenic appeal and tourism is becoming a leading factor in the town's economy. Other major economic forces include the Japanese-owned Alaska Lumber and Pulp Mill, commercial fishing and fish processing, as well as the federal government—the Coast Guard, Forest Service, Alaska Native Health Service, Bureau of Indian Affairs and Sheldon Jackson College.

Government is the economic foundation of the state capital, Juneau, with more than 20,000 residents. In 1978 about 6,017 workers were employed in various branches of borough, state and federal government. Three smaller suburbs—Douglas, across Gastineau Channel on Douglas Island, and Mendenhall Valley and Auke Bay north of Juneau—have prospered from the commercial and government activity of Juneau. Mendenhall Glacier, a major tourist attraction and the only glacier in Southeast accessible by road, deposits icebergs into Mendenhall Lake about 12 miles north of town.

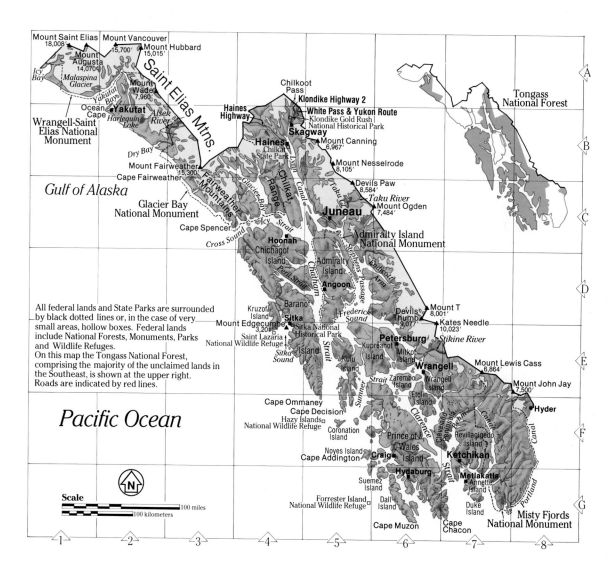

All federal lands and State Parks are surrounded
by black dotted lines or, in the case of very
small areas, hollow boxes. Federal lands
include National Forests, Monuments, Parks
and Wildlife Refuges.
On this map the Tongass National Forest,
comprising the majority of the unclaimed lands in
the Southeast, is shown at the upper right.
Roads are indicated by red lines.

Scale
100 miles
100 kilometers

Discovery of gold in 1880 led to the founding of Juneau. Today the legendary early mines are silent; but rising metal prices have generated a resurgence of mining activity. As in all towns in Southeast, fishing plays an important role in the economy.

Northwest of Juneau lies Glacier Bay, where icebergs calve from 16 active tidewater glaciers and spread throughout myriad bays and inlets of the 3.3-million-acre Glacier Bay National Monument. The small community of Gustavus, nearest to the monument, is connected by a nine-mile road from the airport to monument headquarters at Bartlett Cove.

Until 1979 the monument's icy waterways were a regular summer feeding area for endangered humpback whales, but the whales seemed to have left the area. Some local observers, however, are convinced that the whales' absence is only temporary.

East of Glacier Bay is 60-mile-long Lynn Canal, the passage between the Coast Mountains and the Chilkat Range that provides water access to Haines, on Chilkoot Inlet, and Skagway, near the head of Taiya Inlet.

Originally founded as a Presbyterian mission in 1881, Haines was a mining supply center for various gold rushes until the mid-1920's, as well as a fishing port and salmon canning center. In the early 1900's the U.S. government built the first permanent military base in Alaska at nearby Port Chilkoot. In 1970 Haines and Port Chilkoot merged. Today, with a population of about 1,500, the area is the headquarters of a Native cultural center and home port for an active gill-net fleet.

Because of generally drier weather, compared with the rest of Southeast, agriculture has spurred the economy. The Haines strawberry, developed around the turn of the century by Charles Anway, is exported to many areas of the country.

Leaning dead alders, standing spruce
and some of the lush vegetation at Bartlett Cove
in Glacier Bay National Monument.
(Michio Hoshino)

Fourteen miles north of Haines is Skagway, northern terminus of the Inside Passage; southern terminus of the White Pass & Yukon Route railway and of the Klondike Highway; gateway to the Chilkoot Trail and disembarking point for the thousands of gold miners who swarmed to the Klondike in 1897-98. Today Skagway's 1,000 or so residents rely mostly on tourism. Freight volume on the White Pass has decreased in recent years, prompting a search for alternative uses for the rail equipment. Skagway is rich in gold rush memorabilia and Chilkoot Trail is now part of the Klondike Gold Rush National Historical Park.

The northern neck of Southeast Alaska, a narrow coastal stretch from Glacier Bay to Malaspina Glacier, is characterized by mountains, glaciers and generally rugged terrain. There are few harbors and even fewer signs of human activity between Glacier Bay and Yakutat Bay.

Yakutat, with its harbor on Monti Bay and huge Yakutat Bay just beyond some nearshore islands, is the only community in the area. Fishing supports this mostly Tlingit community of about 500. Across the bay to the north lies the ice mass of Malaspina Glacier, largest in North America. The skyline is dominated by Mount Saint Elias, 18,008 feet, and in the far distance by Canada's Mount Logan, at 19,850 feet the second-highest peak on the continent.

A humpback whale diving in Stephens Passage, an 80-mile-long channel from Portland Island to Frederick Sound, south of Juneau.
(Lou Barr, reprinted from *ALASKA GEOGRAPHIC®*)

15

Below
Ketchikan, population about 14,600, is the first major Alaska community encountered by visitors coming up the Inside Passage from Seattle, hence Ketchikan's nickname, First City.
(Matthew Donohoe)

Left
Some early-day buildings still stand in downtown Wrangell despite two serious fires in this century. Today Wrangell, population about 3,000, thrives on fishing, lumber and tourism.
(Staff, reprinted from *ALASKA GEOGRAPHIC®*)

Below
Aerial photograph of Petersburg, at the north end of the Wrangell Narrows. The community, known as Alaska's "Little Norway," is a fishing center.
(Dick Estelle)

Above
At Shakes Island in Wrangell are some of the oldest Tlingit houseposts. The posts (above right) were carved before 1800 and were moved from the Tlingit village of Kotslitan (Old Wrangell) to Shakes Island in 1869.
(Both photos by Barry Herem, reprinted from *ALASKA*® magazine)

Right
The braided channel of the Stikine River close to its mouth near Wrangell. The river rises in northern British Columbia and flows 400 miles to the sea.
(Staff, reprinted from *ALASKA*® magazine)

Left
John Bobner cuts a Sitka spruce log, a valuable timber species in Southeast.
(Steve McCutcheon)

Below
The freighter, Atlantic Pioneer, *waits at the dock in Metlakatla, on Annette Island. Louisiana Pacific, Ketchikan Division, operates the mill that processes primarily hemlock. A new processing line to handle small hemlock logs, formerly processed into pulp, is expected to be on line this year.*
(S. Forrest Blau)

Right
Piles of wood chips for processing into pulp at the Ketchikan mill.
(Matthew Donohoe)

18

Left

Beautiful Sitka, as seen from Harbor Mountain. This community of about 7,200 was once the capital of Russian America and is now a center for fishing, timber and pulp processing, education and tourism.
(Ed Cooper)

Below

The spires and domes of Saint Michael's Cathedral in Sitka. The original structure, which was built in 1844-48, burned in 1966. The doors and many of the icons were saved, however, and the church has since been rebuilt.
(Mark Kelley)

19

Left
Juneau, the state capital, spreads out on the mainland on the far side of 19-mile-long Gastineau Channel. The community of Douglas, on Douglas Island, is in the foreground.
(William Bacon III)

Below
Mendenhall Glacier and Lake viewed from the visitor center, 13 miles north of Juneau. Named for Professor Thomas Corwin Mendenhall, a superintendent of the U.S. Coast & Geodetic Survey, the glacier is accessible by road and is a major scenic attraction.
(John Helle, reprinted from *ALASKA GEOGRAPHIC®*)

Above
Cruise ships and a small plane that flies sightseers over the Juneau Icefield lie at rest at the Juneau harbor.
(Mark M. Smith)

Right
The Governor's Mansion in Juneau, completed in 1913, was built and furnished for $40,000.
(Ed Cooper)

Left
For years life for many Southeasterners revolved around fishing. Ketchikan billed itself as the salmon capital of the world. While not as important as it used to be, fishing is still a major economic force in Southeast. This fisherman is preparing to gaff a king salmon.
(Matthew Donohoe)

Lower left
Fishermen work a trap at Metlakatla, on Annette Island. Only Natives are allowed to operate traps.
(Kirk Mathews)

Below
Old rooming houses and other buildings line the shore of Port Alexander, a fishing community near the southern tip of Baranof Island.
(Charlie Ott)

Left
The first salmon cannery in Alaska opened in Klawock in 1868 and the village has maintained its ties with the fishing industry ever since. Today about 323 residents, primarily Tlingits, live in this community on the west side of Prince of Wales Island.
(Stephen Hilson, reprinted from *ALASKA GEOGRAPHIC®*)

Below
The serene waters of Elfin Cove, near the north tip of Chichagof Island, reflect the fishing boats and buildings of the small community with the same name on the east shore of the cove.
(Jim Nilsen)

Left
Both black and brown/grizzly bears inhabit Southeast. This black bear was photographed near the North Arm of Dundas Bay in Glacier Bay National Monument.
(William Boehm)

Below
Sitka blacktail deer swim across a narrow channel in Olga Strait, near Sitka.
(Harold Wahlman, reprinted from *Alaska: A Pictorial Geography*)

Right
The fishing community of Angoon, the majority of whose 527 inhabitants are Tlingit Indians, is the only permanent settlement on Admiralty Island in central Southeast.
(Stephen Hilson, reprinted from *ALASKA GEOGRAPHIC®*)

Right
Historic Skagway, at the north end of Taiya Inlet on Lynn Canal, is the oldest incorporated city in Alaska and a year-round port. Skagway owes its beginning to the Klondike gold rush when miners seeking their fortune in the gold fields near Dawson, Yukon Territory, disembarked at Skagway and Dyea before heading over Chilkoot Pass and White Pass. An eight-block district in the heart of Skagway has been designated as a portion of the Klondike Gold Rush National Historical Park, which commemorates the great stampede.
(George Wuerthner)

Left
Originally known as Fort William H. Seward, Chilkoot Barracks, as it became known in the 1920's, was one of five early military posts built in Alaska. The barracks were maintained until the 1940's. Several years ago the site was purchased by a World War II veterans group that became interested in preserving Native culture. The site is now the headquarters of Alaska Indian Arts, Inc. In 1972 Chilkoot Barracks was designated a national historic site and again became officially known as Fort William H. Seward.
(George Wuerthner)

Right
Bergs from Muir Glacier drift out Muir Inlet in Glacier Bay National Monument on their way to the sea.
(Michio Hoshino)

26

Left
A section of Hubbard Glacier calves into Disenchantment Bay east of Yakutat. Scientists are studying the movement of the glacier, named for Gardiner G. Hubbard, the first president of the National Geographic Society, to see if a forward thrust of the glacier might cut off Russell Fiord from Disenchantment Bay.
(Steve McCutcheon)

Right
The isolated Pacific coast south of Yakutat. Few people visit this area of Alaska where the lush coastal vegetation backs against the glaciers of the Saint Elias and Fairweather mountains.
(Bill Harrigan)

Southcentral/ Gulf Coast

Southcentral/Gulf Coast has some of the most rugged terrain in Alaska and the state's biggest population center. Sandwiched between lofty peaks of the Alaska Range and the Gulf of Alaska, the region ranges west from the Yakutat area to include Kodiak Island, the Kenai Peninsula and Cook Inlet.

Southcentral's mainland is a roller coaster topography of high mountains and broad river valleys. To the east the Copper, Chitina and Matanuska rivers are hemmed in by the Chugach, Wrangell and Talkeetna mountains and the crest of the Alaska Range. To the west the Susitna River flows into the muddy upper reaches of Cook Inlet, a 220-mile-long body of water between the Kenai Mountains and Aleutian Range. The other major indentation in the mainland is Prince William Sound, a 15,000-square-mile maze of water, ice and islands. The Kodiak Archipelago extends southwest from the Kenai Peninsula and shields the western flank of the mainland, to some extent, from Gulf of Alaska storms. Kodiak Island, at 3,588 square miles, ranks as the state's largest island.

The climate is maritime—rain and fog—with mild temperature fluctuations. Nearer the mountains, the climate becomes transitional and temperature changes are greater and the climate is generally harsher. In Anchorage, January temperatures average 13°F; July temperatures average 57°F. Protected by the Chugach and Kenai mountains from the moisture-laden clouds from the gulf, Anchorage averages about 15 inches of precipitation annually. However, at Whittier, on the coast, annual average precipitation is 175 inches. Portage, 13 miles away, receives 58 inches a year.

Variable terrain and climate provide suitable habitat for an assortment of plants and wildlife. The moisture-demanding vegetation of Southeast continues along the coast to the Kenai Peninsula and Kodiak. Sitka spruce and western hemlock dominate the coastal forests. Farther inland birch, alder and aspen are the primary species. At higher elevations the forests give way to subalpine brush thickets, fields of wild flowers, berries and alpine meadows. Major river valleys have stands of black cottonwood. Chugach National Forest, created in 1907, encompasses 4.7 million acres of Southcentral's forests.

Variety also characterizes Southcentral's animal populations. Big game species abound. Brown/grizzly bears, the only large mammal native to Kodiak Island, are equally at home in portions of the Matanuska and Susitna valleys and on the flats on the west side of Cook Inlet. Sitka blacktail deer, reindeer, mountain goats and Dall sheep have been introduced to Kodiak, and elk to nearby Afognak Island. Moose thrive on the Kenai National Moose Range in parts of the Matanuska, Susitna and Copper river valleys. Mountain goats roam the sheer cliffs of Prince William Sound, the Kenai Mountains and Kodiak Island. Dall sheep are found in the Talkeetna, Wrangell and Chugach mountains, slopes of the Alaska Range and inland peaks of the Kenai Mountains. The Kenai Peninsula also supports two separate bands of caribou: one on the flats of the western peninsula and one in the mountains. Sitka blacktail deer and black and brown/grizzly bears inhabit the coastal forests of Prince William Sound. Wolves survive on the Kenai Peninsula, in the Nelchina basin, the Copper River valley, the Eagle River valley near Anchorage, and in the rolling country northwest of Cook Inlet.

Smaller mammals in the Southcentral/Gulf Coast region include lynx, pine marten, weasels, beaver, muskrat, mink, red foxes, land otters, porcupines, wolverines, snowshoe hares, shrews, voles and lemmings. Southcentral has congregations of bald and golden eagles, hawks and falcons, and an over-

Aerial view of the fishing community of Cordova, population 2,780, with Orca Inlet in the foreground and Eyak Lake in the background.
(Steve McCutcheon)

32

whelming number of shorebirds and waterfowl. The world's population of dusky Canada geese summer on the Copper River flats, and rare trumpeter swans nest on the Kenai Peninsula and near the Copper River.

The rich Gulf Coast waters support shellfish populations of crabs, shrimp and clams. Salmon, herring, cod, Dolly Varden and cutthroat trout abound and nourish, in turn, harbor and Dall porpoise and killer whales. Largest marine mammals in the area are the baleen whales—humpbacks, fins and minkes—which feed on krill and other marine invertebrates that thrive in the nutrient-rich waters.

Anchorage is the center of Alaska's transportation complex. More than a dozen major domestic and foreign air carriers land at Anchorage International, and Lake Hood, just across the road, is the largest seaplane base in the world.

Anchorage began as a railroad construction camp and the Alaska Railroad is still an important carrier of passengers and freight between Anchorage and Fairbanks. Freight routes extend to Seward on the Kenai Peninsula and the state operates a spur line from Anchorage to Whittier that transports passengers and vehicles. From Whittier passengers can board the M.V. *Bartlett*, a state ferry which connects Whittier, Valdez and Cordova. Another ferry, the M.V. *Tustumena,* serves Seward, Homer, Seldovia, Kodiak, Port Lions, King Cove and Sand Point, as well as Valdez and Cordova.

Cruise ship traffic in Alaska is confined almost entirely to Southeast, but occasionally ships call at Anchorage en route to the Pribilof Islands or other Bering Sea coast ports.

Alaska is not known for its extensive highway networks but there are eight to ten major routes and two of them pass through Anchorage. The Seward Highway and its offshoot, the Sterling, serve the Kenai Peninsula. The Seward runs south from Anchorage to Seward on Resurrection Bay on the east side of the peninsula (127 miles). The Sterling branches off from the Seward near Kenai Lake and extends west and

south for 136 miles to Homer. The Glenn Highway heads northeast from Anchorage to Glennallen and on to the Alaska Highway (345 miles). About 35 miles out from Anchorage the George Parks Highway meets the Glenn. The Parks, a recent addition to the state's highway system, was completed in 1971 and runs 358 miles from Anchorage to Fairbanks past Mount McKinley. The Richardson Highway, the region's other major route, extends north 266 miles from Valdez to Delta Junction on the Alaska Highway. The original road went all the way to Fairbanks but a portion of the Richardson was absorbed by the Alaska Highway with its construction in the 1940's.

At the eastern edge of the Southcentral/Gulf Coast region is the Wrangell-Saint Elias National Monument, designated in 1978 by President Carter.

The coast from Icy Bay to the Copper River Delta is vegetated flatlands pushed seaward by the Robinson Mountains and the large glaciers that flow from the

Thousands of birds use the Copper River Delta as a breeding ground or a rest stop for flights farther north. The Copper River heads on the north side of the Wrangell Mountains and flows south 250 miles through the Chugach Mountains to the Gulf of Alaska.
(Rose Arvidson)

33

Bagley Icefield in the Chugach Mountains. The coastline offers few refuges from the fury of the Gulf of Alaska and aside from a few families living near Yakataga, the area is relatively uninhabited.

The Copper River, historic gateway to the rich mineral deposits of the Wrangell Mountains, drains into the Gulf of Alaska east of Cordova. The mud flats of the river's delta are a major landfall for migrating shorebirds and waterfowl. Salmon, too, use the river as a route to spawning grounds.

At Hinchinbrook Entrance, the Gulf of Alaska merges with Prince William Sound, home of major salmon fishery, crabbing and shrimping industries. Cordova, population 2,780, is the primary fishing port for the eastern sound. In the 1964 earthquake the townsite rose six to seven feet which left the port facilities high and dry. The Army Corps of Engineers dredged the harbor and built a bulkhead to contain the dredge material. The mud solidified and formed a flat area suitable for new construction. Canneries at Cordova process tanner, king and Dungeness crabs; king, red, coho, chum and pink salmon; razor clams, halibut and herring. The 50-mile Copper River Highway leads east from town past Eyak Lake, and the Sheridan and Sherman glaciers to the Copper River.

Farther into Prince William Sound, on Port Valdez, is Valdez, the southern terminus of the trans-Alaska pipeline, which runs 800 miles from Prudhoe Bay oil fields in the Arctic Ocean. The town, population 4,481, has recovered from the devastation of the Good Friday earthquake and now relies on support activities for the pipeline terminal and on construction and operation of an oil refinery. The ice-free port of Valdez with its connection to the Richardson Highway is the shortest route to Interior Alaska from Lower 48 ports. Shipment of goods along this route stimulates additional revenue as does commercial salmon fishing and tourism.

Columbia Glacier, west of Valdez, is a major visitor attraction. The M.V. *Bartlett* and tour boats from

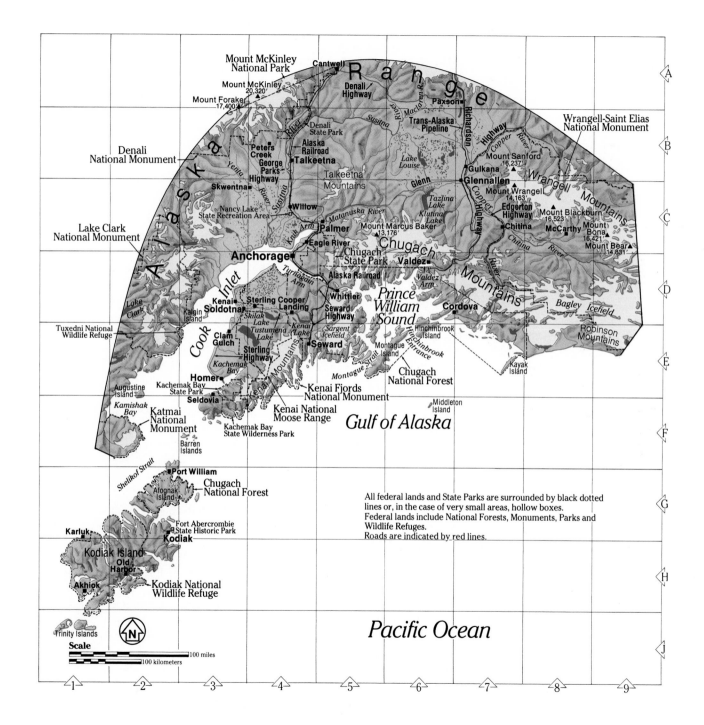

All federal lands and State Parks are surrounded by black dotted lines or, in the case of very small areas, hollow boxes.
Federal lands include National Forests, Monuments, Parks and Wildlife Refuges.
Roads are indicated by red lines.

Valdez and Whittier take visitors into Columbia Bay to view the glacier, whose face ranges from 164 to 262 feet in height, and the harbor seals, bald eagles, black-legged kittiwakes and gulls that feed on the rich marine life.

West of the 440-square-mile mass of Columbia Glacier lies the port of Whittier, population 356, the hub of small boat traffic for western Prince William Sound. Many commercial fishermen operate out of Cordova but when the salmon runs increase in the western sound in late June and July, skippers from Cordova and even from Seward transfer their operations to Whittier.

Thickly forested bays and sheer cliffs characterize the Gulf Coast south and west of Whittier as far as Resurrection Bay and the port of Seward. Fishing, a lumbermill and government-related activities provide jobs for many of the town's residents. Seward's small-boat harbor, modern and well equipped, is home port for numerous charter fishing vessels. Sightseeing excursions into Resurrection Bay to offshore islands such as the Chiswells with their large Steller sea lion colonies and thousands of sea birds, and to Aialik Bay, notable for its tidewater glaciers and wildlife, are generating increased tourist dollars. Seward is also a jumping-off point for trips into Kenai Fjords National Monument. Flightseeing trips are available over Resurrection Bay and the Harding Icefield.

The southern end of the Kenai Peninsula offers a challenge to adventurers willing to tackle its rugged terrain and sometimes rough coastal waters. Portlock, near the peninsula's tip, was once a small fishing community but the cannery closed and the townsite was abandoned. English Bay, Port Graham and the larger community of Seldovia, population 612, all on the south side of Kachemak Bay, depend on fishing, fish processing and to a lesser extent, lumbering and tourism.

The Sterling Highway ends on the north shore of Kachemak Bay at the fishing and tourist community of Homer. Prospector Homer Pennock earned his place in history by giving his name to a site near the end of 4.5-mile-long Homer Spit where the town and first post office were located. The commercial center of Homer has moved back from the spit over the years and the main downtown streets now extend out from a core area on a bluff above Kachemak Bay.

A comparatively mild climate and relatively quiet living have attracted artists and craftspeople who live side by side with fishermen, businessmen and tradesmen. Processing shrimp, crab, halibut and salmon in season keep the canneries busy. Eventually the community plans to develop a bottom fish industry. Rich deposits of coal—collected for home use by some local residents—lie just to the north of Homer. Commercial extraction of the fossil fuel would give the economy an additional boost.

North of Homer along the Sterling Highway are several small beach-front communities, some of which cluster around a cannery. The area is popular with visitors from Anchorage because the clam digging and fishing are great.

Kenai, neighboring North Kenai and Soldotna plus a few smaller settlements, comprise the industrial heart of the Kenai Peninsula. Kenai, population 5,364, is the largest town on the peninsula. Oil and gas turn the economic wheels of Kenai: drilling rigs are located offshore. Collier Carbon and Chemical Plant produces ammonia and urea for fertilizer; Phillips LNG ships liquefied gas to Japan; and Tesoro and Standard Oil refineries employ hundreds of workers. Nearby Nikiski has been chosen as the site for a natural gas liquefaction plant. Besides the oil beneath its muddy bottom, Cook Inlet waters yielded enough salmon in 1979 to keep Kenai Packers and several other processors operating full steam.

The Kenai Peninsula's interior is moose country, 1.7 million acres of which lie in the Kenai National Moose Range. Established in 1941, the range has become a popular area for hunters, hikers, sport fishermen, canoeists, kayakers, backpackers—for all outdoor enthusiasts.

College Fiord, an estuary in Prince William Sound about 63 miles east of Anchorage, extends 18 miles northeast off Port Wells. The Harriman Alaska Expedition first named many of the surrounding glaciers for American colleges, then named the fiord.

The expedition was organized and sponsored by Edward Henry Harriman of New York who invited about 30 scientific men to go to Alaska aboard the steamer George W. Elder in the summer of 1899 to explore, conduct surveys and collect specimens. Leaving Seattle on July 1, they cruised about 9,000 miles and named several other geographic features, including Harriman Glacier and Fiord, before returning on August 31.

Baltimore Glacier was named later—in 1908—but in the college-naming tradition, by U.S. Grant and D.F. Higgins for "the Woman's College of Baltimore, now Goucher College."

Eliot Glacier, which heads on Mount Marcus Baker and trends seven miles to Harvard Glacier, was named two years later—in 1910—by Lawrence Martin of a National Geographic Society expedition for Charles William Eliot, a former Harvard president. Martin also named Lowell (for Abbot Lawrence Lowell, another Harvard president) and Downer Glacier (for Milwaukee-Downer College for Women in Milwaukee, Wisconsin).

Mount Marcus Baker was named even later—in 1924—by A.H. Brooks for a cartographer with the U.S. Coast & Geodetic Survey and the U.S. Geological Survey.

Just out of the photograph to the left are Barnard and Holyoke glaciers.
(Steve McCutcheon)

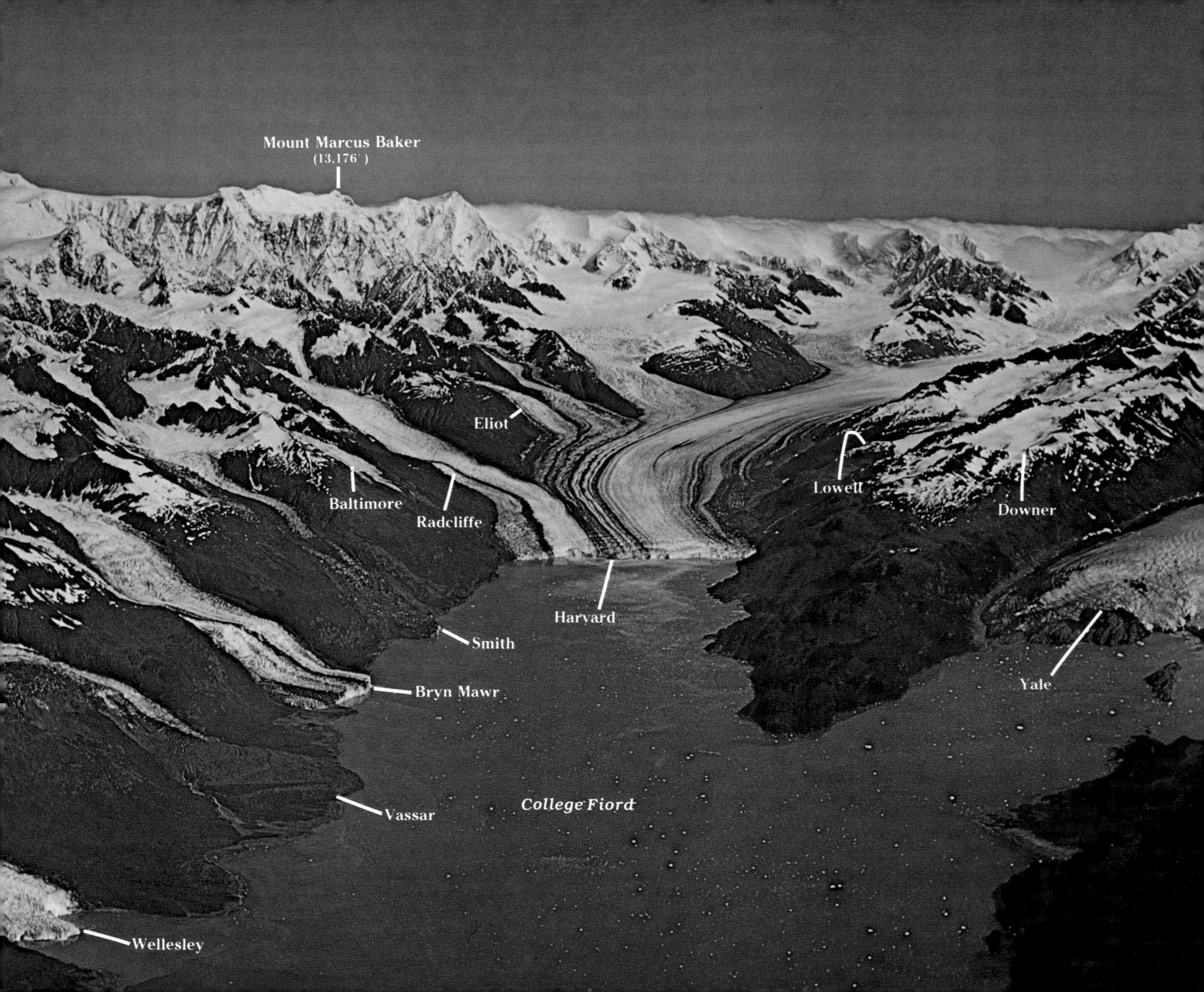

Mount Marcus Baker
(13,176´)

Eliot

Baltimore

Radcliffe

Lowell

Downer

Harvard

Smith

Bryn Mawr

Yale

Vassar

College Fiord

Wellesley

Near Portage at the head of Turnagain Arm the narrow neck of the peninsula joins the Southcentral mainland. Portage Glacier, at the end of a short spur off the Seward Highway, attracts almost as many sightseers as Mount McKinley.

About 47 miles north of Portage sprawls Anchorage, population about 200,000, Alaska's largest city and hub of commerce, industry, transportation and culture for the region and the state. A fast-growing boom town, Anchorage got its start from railroad construction, grew dramatically with establishment of nearby military facilities during World War II, and continues to expand over the lowland where Knik Arm and Turnagain Arm, the gaping jaws of upper Cook Inlet, converge.

Urban sprawl has pushed Anchorage into Mountain View, Muldoon, Spenard, South Anchorage. Eagle River, a quick drive out the Glenn Highway to just beyond the Army's Fort Richardson and the Air Force's Elmendorf, is a residential retreat for many Anchorage workers. A city bus system, financial services, universities, cultural events, medical facilities, towering hotels and award-winning restaurants . . . Anchorage has most everything the Lower 48 cities offer and then some. Dog mushers race through downtown streets during the Anchorage Fur Rendezvous, some office workers cross-country ski along a 75-mile network of trails to beat the morning and afternoon traffic jams that can plague the city's main thoroughfare. On some nights the wispy drapes of the northern lights can be seen over Anchorage. And what Lower 48 city can boast wild moose munching on backyard bushes, or a wolf pack in a valley just beyond the city limits?

Anchorage is made up of people from almost everywhere and anywhere. A few are even from Anchorage. Originally part of the homeland of the Tanaina branch of Athabascan Indians, Anchorage has welcomed all.

The Port of Anchorage handles a major portion of the state's marine shipping volume. Several firms run scheduled containership and barge service to the Lower 48 and at least one company has scheduled service to the Orient. Like all modern cities, Anchorage has shopping malls of all sizes throughout the city.

Several regional Native corporations maintain offices in Anchorage and the federal government opened a new building in 1979.

Satellite transmissions bring Anchorage closer to Outside news sources. Four television and several radio stations and two daily newspapers keep Anchoragites informed.

The Alaska Range stretches across the horizon north of Anchorage. The Talkeetna Mountains rise in the northeast; the broad birch and willow forests of the Susitna lie to the northwest. Spreading out from where the Glenn and George Parks highways converge is the Matanuska Valley, agricultural heartland of Alaska. A variety of crops—both grain and horticultural—grow in the rich soil. New communities have come to life along the Parks Highway with the proposed move of the state capital to nearby Willow.

South of the Kenai Peninsula lie the 16 major islands of the Kodiak Archipelago. Kodiak is synonymous with bears and fish. Kodiak National Wildlife Refuge covers much of Kodiak Island itself. The brown/grizzly bears for which the island is renowned are especially numerous in the western and southern reaches of the island but they also exist in the north where cattle graze.

Kodiak's streams, some of which can be reached by road, offer excellent trout and salmon fishing. But commercial fishing is king . . . the lifeblood of an economy that harvests millions of pounds of crab, shrimp, halibut, salmon, scallops and herring. Bottom fishing, a new piece of the commercial fishing pie, is certain to play an important role in the future.

Logging is a possibility on neighboring Afognak Island once much of the land is transferred to the regional Native corporation. Kodiak is also home to the largest Coast Guard base in the state.

Above
Sea lions swim near Point Elrington at the south end of Elrington Island in Prince William Sound.
(Jana Craighead, reprinted from *ALASKA*® magazine)

40

Left
The tiny village of Tatitlek,
population 111, clings to the
shores of Prince William Sound
below Copper Mountain, about
40 miles northwest of Cordova.
(Nancy Simmerman)

Lower left
The neatly organized community
of Valdez, population 4,481.
The town was severely damaged
in the 1964 earthquake and
its citizens voted to move the
town site to a safer location
before rebuilding.
(Steve McCutcheon)

Right
A state ferry and several tour
boats take visitors past Columbia
Glacier, a major attraction in
Prince William Sound. Only the
lower 12 miles of the glacier's
41-mile total length can be seen
from Columbia Bay.
(Nancy Simmerman)

Left
Bearberry adds a touch of red to the tundra carpet of Little O'Malley Peak in Chugach State Park.
(Charlotte Casey, Staff)

Left
Layers of peaks stack together in this telephoto view of the Chugach Mountains, taken in April from the summit of O'Malley Peak, not far from Anchorage in the Chugach Mountains.
(John Dancer)

Right
The Matanuska Glacier extends 27 miles from its head in the Chugach Mountains to a stream that flows into the Matanuska River 46 miles northeast of Palmer.
(Ed Cooper)

Aerial view of the Matanuska Valley, looking north over Palmer. The Talkeetna Mountains loom on the horizon and at center and right is the Matanuska River.
(Alan C. Paulson)

Left
Peaks of the Alaska Range near Cathedral Spires about 60 miles southwest of the McKinley summit are illuminated by a late evening sun in this photo taken from a small plane flying at 9,000 feet.
(Staff)

Lower left
Four oil drilling platforms are visible in this photo taken in upper Cook Inlet. Gas that is released when the oil is brought to the surface is burned off, or flared.
(Steve McCutcheon)

Left
Five-year-old Andy Grendahl lands his first king salmon at Lake Creek, which flows into the Yentna River 58 miles northwest of Anchorage.
(Jim Thiele)

Right
Aerial view of Anchorage. The downtown shopping area is in the center, bordered on the left by Ship Creek and on the right by the Park Strip, a block-wide and several-block-long greenbelt. Facilities for the Port of Anchorage are at the extreme left. The Chugach Mountains rise in the distance.
(North Pacific Aerial Surveys)

Above
Downtown Anchorage, looking west across Cook Inlet to the peaks of the Aleutian Range. Anchorage is Alaska's largest city and the commercial and transportation center for Southcentral.
(George Herben)

Right
The major winter event for Anchorage, Fur Rendezvous, offers a variety of indoor and outdoor events including world championship sled dog races. Here Roland Lombard, one of the most successful mushers, guides his team along the men's championship course.
(Gary Lackie)

Left
A bore tide surges up Turnagain Arm. Tides can reach 30 feet in 6 hours along the arm.
(Bob Cellers)

Left
Grasses grow in the tide flats along Turnagain Arm southeast of Anchorage.
(Ed Cooper)

Below
Early morning sun in November lights icebergs in Portage Lake near the head of Turnagain Arm. Portage Glacier is hidden by the fog.
(Nancy Simmerman)

49

Below
The area near Clam Gulch on the Cook Inlet shore of the Kenai Peninsula is a popular spot for clam diggers. The peaks of the Aleutian Range rise in the distance across Cook Inlet.
(Nancy Simmerman)

Left
Seward, on Resurrection Bay, celebrates the Fourth of July in grand style. A grueling run up 3,022-foot Mount Marathon is just one of the events which attracts hundreds of visitors.
(John Warden, reprinted from *The MILEPOST®*)

Right
Kenai Lake extends southwest 24 miles from the Kenai River to the mouth of Snow River, 22 miles northwest of Seward.
(John Warden)

Above

The Homer Spit reaches out 4.5 miles from the north shore of Kachemak Bay at Homer. Several fishing-related facilities and a small-boat harbor line the shores of the spit.
(Charlotte Casey, Staff)

Right

The fishing community of Seldovia, population 612, spreads out along the east shore of Seldovia Bay, 16 miles southwest of Homer. A state ferry connects the town with other Southcentral/Gulf Coast ports.
(Karen Donelson)

Left
Wildlife in Southcentral is varied and sometimes amusing. These two brown/grizzly bears are relaxing near McNeil River, a state game sanctuary on the west side of Cook Inlet.
(Larry Aumiller)

Below
Midwinter light casts a pinkish glow on Augustine Island in lower Cook Inlet, 70 miles southwest of Homer. The volcanic island last erupted in late January and early February, 1976.
(Art Kennedy, reprinted from *ALASKA*® magazine)

Right
The harbor at Kodiak, one of the top fishing ports in the country.
(Charlotte Casey, Staff)

Interior

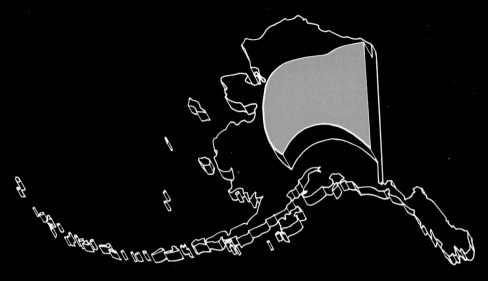

*Kayakers paddle
through calm waters of
Wonder Lake in Mount
McKinley National Park.
Peaks of the Alaska
Range loom in
the distance.*
(Jim Shives)

For some the Interior is the "real" Alaska. Low rolling hills, braided streams flowing into meandering rivers, forested taiga and treeless tundra, all corralled between the Alaska Range on the south, the Brooks Range on the north, the Canadian border on the east and a transition zone with the Bering Sea coast region on the west.

The Interior is a land of superlatives. On the region's southern border stands Mount McKinley, at 20,320 feet the highest peak on the continent. Alaska's longest river, the Yukon, crosses the region's midsection. The Yukon and its tributaries provided the avenues of exploration which eventually brought trappers and miners into the Interior's immense wilderness.

Low precipitation, wide temperature variations and stagnant air masses typify the continental climate of the region. The mean annual wind speed averages five miles per hour at Fairbanks, where prevailing winds are from the north. In Fairbanks January is the calmest month; May the windiest. In January temperatures in Fairbanks average -11°F; in July the average soars to 60°F. The state's highest temperature, 100°F, was recorded in 1915 at Fort Yukon. Prospect Creek, northeast of Bettles, has the dubious distinction of recording the state's lowest temperature, -80°F, in 1971.

There are two distinct environments in the Interior. In the highlands, below 2,000 feet, and in river valleys, boreal forests (taiga) of white spruce, birch and aspen dominate over stands of balsam poplar and tamarack. In muskeg and bogs, however, the hardy, but stunted, black spruce grows. There are also willow, alder, berries, wild flowers, grasses and sedges.

On the tundra, the region's least productive landscape in terms of plant growth, only those plants that can work their roots into the soil and hang on through cold, heat and wind survive.

A land as vast as the Interior, with many wild areas, can shelter large numbers of big and small mammals, birds and fish. Some of the

prime wildlife habitat has been set aside as national parks, monuments and wildlife refuges.

Mount McKinley National Park and the newly designated Denali National Monument—which surrounds the park on three sides—are the state's major tourist attractions.

On the Interior's eastern border is the Yukon-Charley National Monument, providing necessary habitat for endangered peregrine falcons, other raptors, waterfowl, bear and moose. Nearby Eagle, population 200, has geared up for its nomination for Historic Landmark Status in the National Register of Historic Places with organized tours of numerous historic sites in the area. In addition, the monument preserves the Charley River wilderness watershed.

To the north a portion of the central Brooks Range has been set aside as the Gates of the Arctic National Monument.

Some areas containing crucial wildlife nesting and foraging habitat qualify as national wildlife refuges. Chief among these in the Interior is the Yukon Flats (currently designated a national monument but administered as a wildlife refuge), where the mighty river escapes the confines of its temporarily canyon-rimmed course and spreads out over a wide flood plain for 200 miles, creating a great waterfowl breeding area. From there millions of birds—American wigeons, pintails, green-winged teals, scoters, northern shovelers, scaup, canvasbacks, and numerous other species—migrate to four continents. Large (caribou, moose, grizzly and black bears, and wolves) and small (beavers, muskrats, lynx, snowshoe hares) mammals inhabit the flats, and five species of salmon—mostly king and chum—swim through the waterways seeking their spawning grounds.

Farther west are the proposed Koyukuk, Innoko and Nowitna refuges. And in the southeast corner of the Interior is the proposed Tetlin National Wildlife Refuge. A portion of Birch Creek and segments of some rivers and streams in the Fortymile district bordering Canada meet the criteria for wild and scenic rivers status and have been proposed as such by the Secretary of the Interior.

Transportation in the Interior is chiefly by air or water, although in the eastern Interior, roads—the Elliott, Steese, Taylor, Richardson, George Parks and Alaska highways—play a major role in the movement of goods and people.

Fairbanks, population 25,000, is the focal point for this road system, and serves as the population, commercial, financial and industrial center for the Interior—a region which contains about one-third of

Alaska's territory and about one-fifth of its population.

At neighboring North Pole, population 823, a refinery processes more than 30,000 barrels of crude oil per day. The trans-Alaska pipeline passes near Fairbanks and construction activities for the project were coordinated out of the city. The University of Alaska, at College on the edge of Fairbanks, offers a wide variety of programs, specializing in courses related to the northern environment. The renowned Geophysical Institute on the university's campus serves as a leading source of information on northern phenomena. Nearby, too, is the Army's Fort Wainwright and Eielson Air Force Base.

With rising metal and fuel prices, mining—by individuals and companies—once again is becoming a profitable occupation in the Fairbanks area. The Usibelli Coal Mine near Healy has been operating since the early part of the century and continues to produce high-quality subbituminous coal.

Increased fur prices have encouraged more year-round residents to run traplines. Guiding for hunting has always supported some Interior residents, and now a shift to guiding for wilderness and photography treks is bringing income to an increasing number of guides.

Subsistence is a way of life for many in the Interior, and occasionally residents supplement their hunting, fishing and trapping with temporary jobs in construction or fire fighting.

Some of the larger settlements, such as Galena (population 631), McGrath (population 350), Bettles (population 88), and Arctic Village (population 111), serve as trading centers and jumping-off points for wilderness excursions.

Southeast of Fairbanks along the Tanana River valley is the agricultural center of the Interior. Efforts are being made to grow commercial crops— barley, oats, hay, and potatoes in particular—and the total value of crops, livestock and poultry produced in the Tanana valley in 1978 was more than $1.8 million.

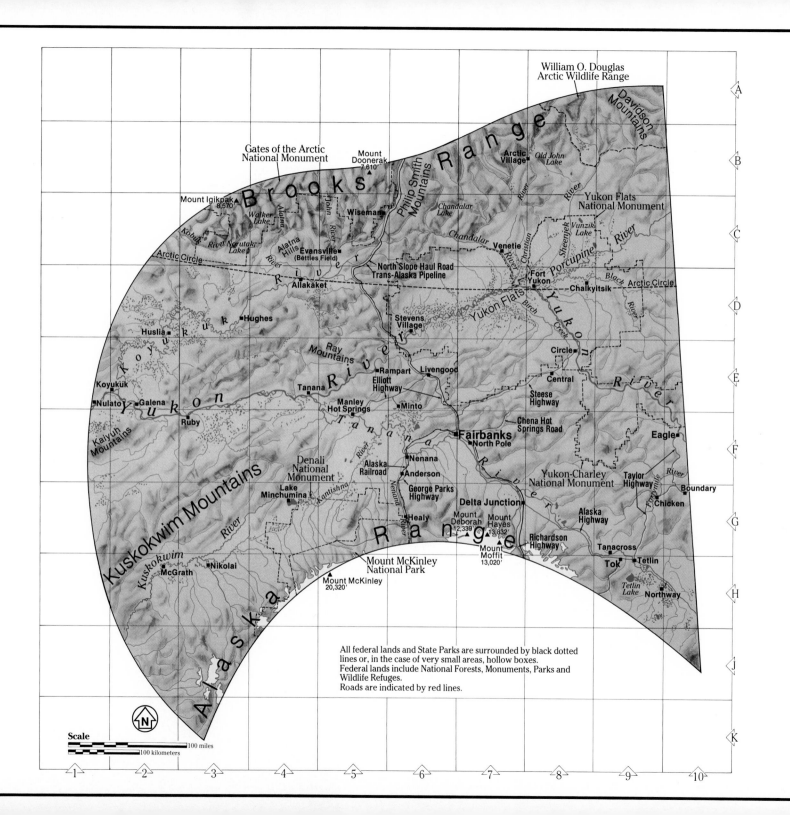

William O. Douglas
Arctic Wildlife Range

Davidson Mountains

Brooks Range

Gates of the Arctic
National Monument

Mount Doonerak
7,610'

Arctic Village

Old John Lake

Philip Smith Mountains

Yukon Flats
National Monument

Mount Igikpak
8,570'

Chandalar Lake

Vunziki Lake

Sheenjek River

Porcupine River

Walker Lake

Alatna

John River

Wiseman

Chandalar

Venetie

Christian River

Kobuk River

Norutakt Lake

Alatna Hills

Evansville
(Bettles Field)

North Slope Haul Road
Trans-Alaska Pipeline

Fort Yukon

Black River

Arctic Circle

Arctic Circle

Allakaket

Chalkyitsik

Koyukuk River

Hughes

Stevens Village

Yukon Flats

Birch Creek

Yukon River

Huslia

Koyukuk

Ray Mountains

Circle

Koyukuk

Rampart

Livengood

Central

Nulato

Galena

Tanana River

Elliott Highway

Steese Highway

River

Kaiyuh Mountains

Ruby

Manley Hot Springs

Minto

Chena Hot Springs Road

Eagle

Tanana

Fairbanks

North Pole

Kuskokwim Mountains

Denali National Monument

Alaska Railroad

Nenana

Yukon-Charley National Monument

Taylor Highway

Boundary

Lake Minchumina

Kantishna River

Anderson

George Parks Highway

Delta Junction

Chicken

Alaska Highway

McGrath

Nikolai

Healy

Mount Deborah 12,339'

Mount Hayes 13,832'

Richardson Highway

Tanacross

Kuskokwim River

Mount Moffit 13,020'

Tetlin

Alaska Range

Mount McKinley National Park

Tok

Mount McKinley 20,320'

Tetlin Lake

Northway

All federal lands and State Parks are surrounded by black dotted lines or, in the case of very small areas, hollow boxes.
Federal lands include National Forests, Monuments, Parks and Wildlife Refuges.
Roads are indicated by red lines.

Scale

100 miles

100 kilometers

A
B
C
D
E
F
G
H
J
K

1 2 3 4 5 6 7 8 9 10

Below
Of the four species of eagles that inhabit Alaska, by far the most common in the Interior is the golden eagle. It preys chiefly on snowshoe hares, marmots, squirrels, rodents and smaller birds.
(Rick McIntyre)

Right
The Yukon breaks free of its canyon-walled channel when it reaches the Yukon Flats and spreads out over a lowland for the next 200 miles, thus creating the perfect breeding ground for millions of waterfowl.
(Dennis and Debbie Miller)

60

Below
The aurora borealis photographed over North Pole, near Fairbanks. The aurora results when gas particles in the upper atmosphere are struck by solar electrons trapped in the earth's magnetic field. Color varies depending on how hard the gas particles are struck.
(Steve Nyberg)

Above
Stands such as these of deciduous birch and aspen mix with white spruce in many of the Interior's forests.
(Robert Langlotz)

Right
In permafrost areas, pure ice—often called ice lenses—lies a few inches below the surface.
(Steve McCutcheon)

Right
A reputation for ferociousness leads many animals to avoid the wolverine, a solitary hunter found in isolated reaches of the Interior.
(William Bacon III)

Below
The huge feet of this immature lynx enable the animal to cope handily with deep snow when chasing snowshoe hares.
(Steve McCutcheon)

Below
Grassland in the Interior supports two bison herds, a large herd near Big Delta and a much smaller herd near Farewell in the western Interior.
(Steve McCutcheon)

Right
Largest member of the deer family is the moose, found throughout the Interior. The velvet has been rubbed off the antlers of this young bull but the blood that nourishes the velvet is still visible.
(Martin Grosnick)

Left
Alaska's most famous geographical feature is Mount McKinley, at 20,320 feet the highest peak in North America. This somewhat familiar view is across Wonder Lake, in Mount McKinley National Park.
(Michio Hoshino)

Below
Sled dogs are an integral part of the McKinley scene. In summer the dogs demonstrate sled pulling and other skills for visitors. In winter the dogs haul rangers and equipment on back country patrol.
(Jim Shives)

Right
Mike Wild, out for a day's skiing, found this ice bridge on a glacier east of Mount McKinley.
(Steven Kaufman)

Left
Aerial view of Fairbanks and the Chena River. Fairbanks has grown from a trading post for nearby gold camps to the second-largest city in Alaska. Nearly 25,000 now live within the city limits.
(Steve McCutcheon)

Below
A gold dredge leaves a trail of tailings as it works the dirt near Fairbanks. Felix Pedro's claim just after the turn of the century heralded the beginnings of the Fairbanks mining district.
(Steve McCutcheon)

Left
Fishing, both commercial, which brings in cash, and subsistence, which brings in needed food, keeps many Interior residents busy during the summer. In 1979, commercial fishermen along the Yukon above Kaltag received approximately $150,000 for their catch—primarily king and chum salmon. This fisherman is checking a set net near Rampart on the Yukon River.
(Harry Walker)

Left
Agriculture in the Interior centers around the Tanana River valley southeast of Fairbanks. Crop value in 1978 totaled more than $1.8 million. Here a stacker shapes the hay into neat piles near Delta Junction.
(Staff)

Above
Low-hanging sun glances off the trans-Alaska pipeline as it winds past 5,600-foot Mount Wiehl (left) and 4,200-foot Sukakpak Mountain in the Dietrich River valley on the south slope of the Brooks Range.
(Steve McCutcheon)

69

Below
Circle Hot Springs, 29 miles southwest of Circle, became a resort when Franklin Leach developed his 160-acre homestead near the springs. Visiting miners who wanted to bathe in the springs occasionally had to chip the ice off the tent flaps when using the bathhouses.
(Sharon Paul, Staff)

Right
The Yukon flows 1,400 miles through Alaska, much of that across the heartland of the Interior. Boats ranging from large river steamers to the tiniest kayaks and rafts have carried passengers and freight from village to village and to remote sites along the river's shores.
(Sharon Paul, Staff)

Opposite
Nenana, population 362, on the Tanana River has served as a major riverboat port for the Interior. The annual Nenana Ice Classic challenges thousands to guess, to the nearest minute, when the Tanana ice will break up at Nenana.
(John and Margaret Ibbotson)

70

Below
Canoeists paddle near shore on the crystal clear waters of Takahula Lake. Just over the low, forested hills bordering the lake's east shore runs the Alatna River, a major tributary of the Koyukuk River.
(Jim Stuart)

Above
Jumping-off point for the Gates of the Arctic and other points in the central Brooks Range is Bettles Field near the confluence of the Koyukuk and John rivers. The lodge at Bettles Field contains some of the few modern conveniences available in the area.
(Gil Mull)

Right
Caribou skins hang to dry at Arctic Village, on the East Fork of the Chandalar River.
(Dennis and Debbie Miller)

Alaska Peninsula & Aleutians

The stone-linked Aleutian Chain forms a slender divider between two of the world's wildest bodies of water, the North Pacific and the stormy Bering Sea, bridging the gap between North America and Asia. Its magnificently faceted, treeless isles are actually crests of an arc of submarine volcanoes, approximately 1,400 miles long and 20 to 60 miles wide, that rise to a maximum height of 9,372 feet above sea level (Shishaldin Volcano on Unimak Island) and 32,472 feet above the ocean floor. On the Pacific side the chain is bordered by the Aleutian Trench, an extraordinary trough more than 2,000 miles long, 50 to 100 miles wide with a maximum depth of over 25,000 feet where continental plates meet beneath the ocean floor. To the north the relatively shallow Bering Sea slopes downward, forming the world's largest known underwater valley, some 249 miles long with a maximum depth of 10,677 feet.

The Aleutians are the longest archipelago of small islands (124) in the world and the greatest arc of active volcanoes in the United States. The volatile span dates back millions of years and is still in a state of flux. Amak, in the eastern region, surfaced about 7,000 years ago and Bogoslof, which emerged in the late 1700's, is still being shaped by volcanic activity and the elements.

Volcanic eruptions and earthquakes remain a common threat as do the tidal waves and landslides they often spawn. At least 26 of the chain's 57 volcanoes have erupted since 1760. But the remoteness of population centers and the severity of climate still discourage geologists, making the chain one of the very few active areas in the world not cataloged by the International Association of Volcanologists.

On April Fools' Day, 1946, the Aleutians suffered a quake that sent waves more than 100 feet high to nearby Unimak, obliterating Scotch Cap lighthouse and killing five coastguardsmen. Seismic sea waves from this quake swept the Pacific at over 500 miles per hour, slamming into Hawaii less than five hours later, killing 159, injuring 163 and causing an estimated $25 million damage.

A seismic warning system was established two years later to protect Hawaiians but seismic work on the Aleutian Chain was not begun in earnest until the 1970's.

The usually conservative U.S. Coast & Geodetic Survey sailing directions declare Aleutian weather the worst in the world. Storm fronts generally move from west to east here but often climatic conditions on the Pacific side differ vastly from those on the Bering side, placing the islands in a continuing weather war. In October of 1977 the remains of tropical storm Harriet slammed into the Aleutians forcing barometric pressure to the lowest ever recorded: 27.35 inches at Adak and off the glass at Atka. Waves from 45 to 50 feet high were reported off Cape Sarichef and several homes were blown off their foundations at Atka.

Measurable precipitation occurs on an average of more than 200 days each year with an annual average of 33.44 inches at Cold Bay on the Alaska Peninsula and 28.85 inches at Shemya in the extreme western Aleutians.

Luckily, Aleutian temperatures are milder than elsewhere in Alaska due to the southerly position and the tempering effect of the surrounding waters. At Shemya temperatures range from 39°F to 53°F in summer and from 28°F to 39°F in winter. The 28.85 inches of precipitation include 57 inches of snow. At Dutch Harbor, near the mainland, temperatures range from 40°F to 60°F in summer and from 27°F to 37°F in winter. The 58 inches of precipitation annually includes 81 inches of snow.

There is little or no permafrost and gardens thrive when unmolested by predators. The islands are treeless except where man has succeeded in nurturing spruce in sheltered valleys. In summer the Aleutians become emerald Edens of grasses studded with a variety of wild flowers.

"The arctic and alpine merge on these islands . . . rosy finches and arctic snow buntings nest practically side by side close to sea level," noted biologist Olaus Murie. The chain is a focal point to which animal life has long come from north and south, east and west, and a melting pot for fauna from two continents.

Although a full census has yet to be made, more than 180 species of birds have been recorded, including a new one listed in 1979.

Marine mammals are attracted to the chain by turbulent seas which produce high nutrient concentrates near the surface and support a rich food chain—plankton, fish and shellfish.

Unimak Island is the natural western limit for caribou, brown/grizzly bear, wolf, wolverine, ground squirrel and weasel. Almost all Aleutian land mammals west of the island's borders were introduced by man: foxes, horses, cattle, sheep, caribou and reindeer, and Norwegian rats.

The Aleutians boast the world's largest range of sea mammals: 23 species counting the now-extinct Steller sea cow. The most continually productive whaling ground in Alaska, the chain has 13 species of cetaceans including the giant bottlenose, Bering Sea beaked and Cuvier's beaked whales.

Until the 1940's naturalists feared the island's sea otters might become extinct but a well-observed ban on hunting (the result of a 1911 international treaty) has brought populations back. Fur seals, which migrate through Aleutian waters en route to the Pribilofs, have also made a healthy comeback after exploitation. Sea lions, once sought for their skins, are now thought to be near maximum population limits, and harbor seals, elephant seals and walrus also now come to the area in increasing numbers.

Vitus Bering, discoverer of Alaska, sighted several

A cruise ship rests at anchor near six-mile-long Aghiyuk Island, northernmost of the Semidi Islands. (Dennis Hellawell)

INDEX TO ALASKA PENINSULA & ALEUTIANS GEOGRAPHIC FEATURES

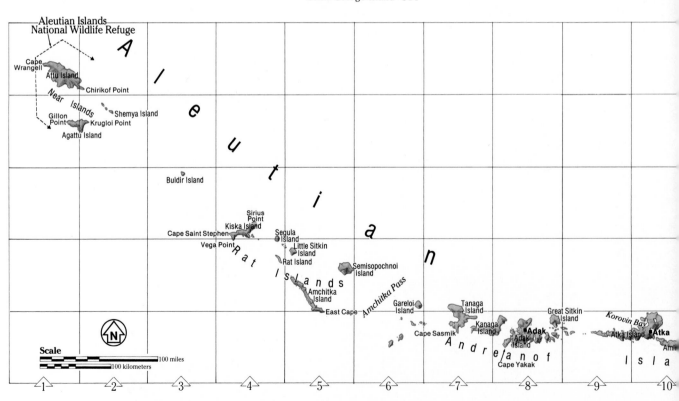

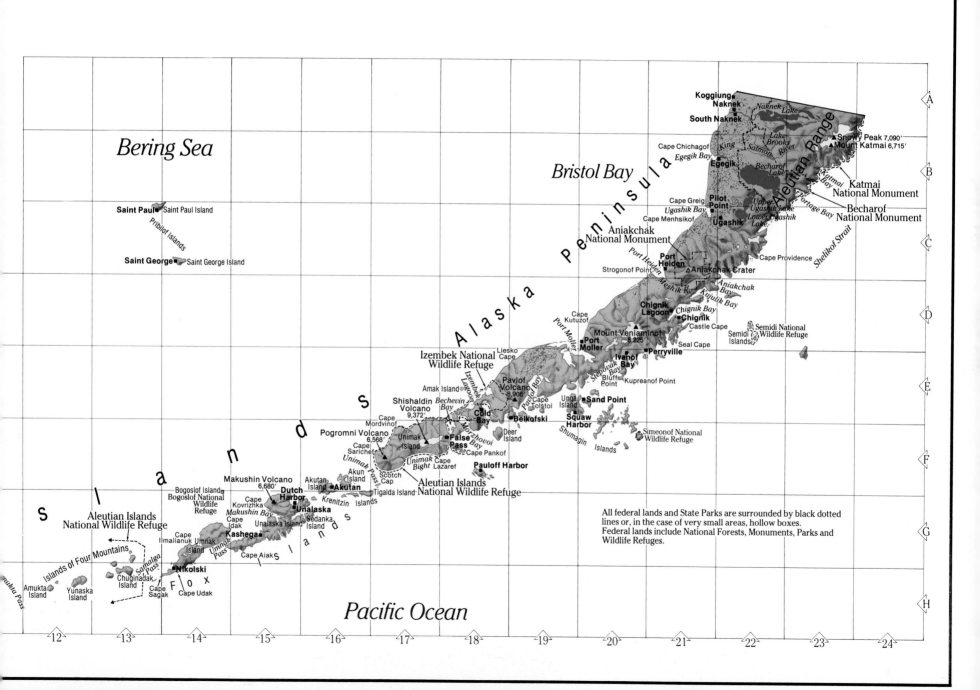

Bering Sea

Bristol Bay

A

Koggiung
Naknek
South Naknek
Naknek Lake
Snowy Peak 7,090'
Mount Katmai 6,715'

Cape Chichagof
Egegik Bay
King Salmon River
Lake Brooks

Aleutian Range

B

Egegik
Becharof Lake

Katmai Bay
Katmai
National Monument

Saint Paul
Saint Paul Island

Cape Greig
Ugashik Bay
Pilot Point
Upper Ugashik Lake
Lower Ugashik Lake

Portage Bay
Becharof
National Monument

Pribilof Islands
Cape Menhsikof
Ugashik

C

Saint George
Saint George Island

Aniakchak
National Monument

Shelikof Strait

Port Heiden
Port Heiden
Cape Providence

Strogonof Point
Aniakchak Crater

Alaska Peninsula

Meshik R.
Aniakchak Bay
Kujulik Bay

Cape Kutuzof
Chignik Lagoon
Chignik Bay
Chignik
Semidi National
Wildlife Refuge

D

Port Moller
Castle Cape
Semidi Islands

Mount Veniaminof
8,225'
Port Moller

Izembek National
Wildlife Refuge
Liesko Cape
Seal Cape
Perryville

Ivanof Bay

Amak Island
Izembek Lagoon

Pavlof Volcano
8,905'
Stepovak Bay
Bluff Point
Kupreanof Point

E

Shishaldin Volcano
9,372'
Bechevin Bay
Cape Tolstoi
Unga Island
Sand Point

Cape Mordvinof
Paul of Bay

Pogromni Volcano
6,568'
Cold Bay
Belkofski
Squaw Harbor

Cape Sarichef
Unimak Island
Morzhovoi Bay
Cape Pankof
Deer Island
Simeonof National
Wildlife Refuge

F

Unimak Pass
Unimak Bight
Scotch Cap
Cape Lazaref
Pauloff Harbor
Shumagin Islands

False Pass

Aleutian Islands
National Wildlife Refuge

Makushin Volcano
6,680'
Akutan Island
Akutan
Krenitzin Islands
Tigalda Island

Bogoslof Island
Bogoslof National
Wildlife Refuge
Dutch Harbor
Cape Kovrizhka
Sedanka Island

All federal lands and State Parks are surrounded by black dotted
lines or, in the case of very small areas, hollow boxes.
Federal lands include National Forests, Monuments, Parks and
Wildlife Refuges.

G

Aleutian Islands
National Wildlife Refuge
Cape Idak
Makushin Bay
Unalaska
Unalaska Island

Cape Ilmalianuk
Umnak Island
Kashega

Islands of Four Mountains
Samalga Pass
Cape Aiak
Umnak Pass

Nikolski

Amukta Pass

Amukta Island
Yunaska Island
Chuginadak Island
Cape Sagak
Cape Udak

FOX

Pacific Ocean

H

12   13   14   15   16   17   18   19   20   21   22   23   24

of the Aleutian Islands on his homeward voyage in 1741. By 1743 concentrated hunting for seal and sea otter furs had begun. Trade with the Aleuts continued after American purchase in 1867 until depletion of animals forced a moratorium on hunting and the declaration of almost the entire archipelago as a federal wildlife refuge in 1913.

During World War II the western chain was invaded and held by the Japanese and the Aleuts were taken captive or evacuated. A year later Americans won back the ground and began pouring $100 million into fortifications. Thousands of men were based at Adak alone, only to pull out at the war's end leaving the islands almost deserted.

Only about half of the original Aleut population (less than 1,000) returned—the rest were either dead or relocated—and there was little left to attract Outsiders. The mail boat was discontinued in the late 1940's and only occasional plane service connected remote villages. Although there was some fishing-related industry in the Aleutians—a cold storage at Sand Point, Popof Island, and fish processing at King Cove—many traditional villages were never resettled; only Nikolski, Akutan, Atka and False Pass were kept alive by a handful of families who existed mainly by subsistence hunting and fishing.

All military bases were closed with the exception of Adak, which the Army Air Force reduced to house-keeping status. Sprawling facilities at Attu and a smaller unit at Sarichef were transferred to the Coast Guard but manned only by small staffs. During the cold war a top secret military installation was opened at Shemya; DEW line sites were built at Sarichef and Nikolski. Adak was transferred to the Navy, which made the base its state headquarters. Adak has since become the chain's largest settlement—at peak times accommodating about 5,000 troops, dependents and support personnel.

There was a building boom at Amchitka during the mid-1960's with the multimillion-dollar Atomic Energy Commission testing program, but most of the

work fell to Outsiders. Area residents protested the experiments and were relieved when the operation closed after three massive tests.

Activity picked up again with enactment in 1976 of a 200-mile fishing limit excluding foreign fleets from American waters. Unalaska, previously not listed in the National Marine Fisheries Service count of dollar values and pounds landed, became the top port in the nation in 1978. Crab catch for that year was worth $99.7 million, and there were 14 processors in operation and half a dozen in neighboring Akutan.

The boom is mainly king crab. Tanner crab (marketed as snow crab) is also important, and a promising bottom fish market is about to be tested. Many multimillion-dollar boats have already been built for the area—utilized now in fishing for salmon, crab, herring and shrimp—ready to convert for bottom fishing when that market ripens. Planners are talking in terms of several shore-based processing plants that will hire many thousands of people. The boom has already had incredible impact on Unalaska, a town with an estimated 619 permanent residents that swells to over 5,000 during the season. Through the congressional land claims settlement, almost all the land in private hands belongs to Natives, and although most despair at the interruption of their tranquil lifestyle, their economic future appears among the most promising in the state.

Unlike Unalaska, Akutan (population 69) has no local fleet, and local government has yet to find a way to tax floating processors; however, jobs are no longer a major problem in that remote village. By 1978 Sand Point (population 829), which has a much

Fresh snowfall glistens on the 4,800-foot Aghileen Pinnacles near Cold Bay at the tip of the Alaska Peninsula. The peaks on the horizon are, from left, Frosty, 5,784 feet and on the mainland; Roundtop, 6,140 feet, Isanotski, 8,025 feet, and Shishaldin, 9,372 feet, all on Unimak Island.
(John Sarvis)

higher percentage of locally owned boats than Unalaska, boasted the second-largest per capita income of any Alaska small town, and peninsula-based King Cove (population 734) is not far behind. The reopening of the long-closed False Pass salmon cannery in 1977 gave that small community (population 55) a new economic boost.

Practically no impact from the boom has been felt at Nikolski (population 56) or Atka (population 92), the most remote village in the state, but long-wanted government housing and public works programs have given these areas new life and some form of industry may follow.

Transportation to and among the Aleutians is infrequent and expensive. Rough flying weather and extraordinary operational costs due to small populations combine to give Reeve Aleutian Airways, Inc., the distinction of flying the most expensive air miles in America. Atka has no scheduled air service and it has no runway. Akutan likewise has no airstrip but is close enough to Unalaska for service by floatplane. The seasonally busy strip at Unalaska is unpaved and only 4,100 feet long, too short for most jets.

Freight service by sea is irregular and there is no inter-island marine transport system.

Further development may be expected as the oil industry eyes offshore waters of the eastern chain; initial leasing procedure is scheduled to start in 1981. Onshore mineral wealth appears to be minimal, but potential for geothermal energy is also being explored and may one day be utilized if population growth warrants.

A fledgling tourist industry—now mainly bird watchers and a few sportsmen—may be expected to grow, especially if World War II battlefields become national monuments as is currently being considered. For now, however, most of the chain remains a wildlife sanctuary—and the majority of permanent residents, addicted to the peace and wild beauty of the islands, will be hard put if given the option for further growth and development.

Above
A brown/grizzly bear waits for his next salmon dinner in Katmai National Monument. The glaucous-winged gulls in the background will readily clean up any scraps left by the bear.
(Martin Grosnick)

Right
On June 6, 1912, 2.5 cubic miles of ash was ejected from Novarupta volcano near Mount Katmai in what some consider to be the second-greatest volcanic eruption in recorded history. More than 40 square miles of the valley near the eruption site were covered with ash, sometimes to depths of 300 feet. This valley was named Valley of Ten Thousand Smokes because there were so many fumaroles still emitting vapors when scientists first arrived to explore the eruption site. The ground has since cooled.
(Michio Hoshino)

Created in 1960, Izembek
National Wildlife Refuge on the
Alaska Peninsula contains
320,801 acres. The continent's
entire brant population
feeds here as do many other
species of waterfowl. These three
photos were all taken in the
refuge. From the top, a harbor
seal resting on a sand bar at low
tide near Cape Glazenap at
the west entrance to Applegate
Cove / Flocks of sanderlings and
rock sandpipers flying along a
beach at Neumann Island. /
Barren Ground caribou bulls,
their antlers still covered with
velvet, at Moffett Point.
(All photos by John Sarvis; center photo
reprinted from *ALASKA*® magazine)

Left
A little over 10 years ago, about 41 persons lived in the village of False Pass on the east end of Unimak Island. The salmon cannery was closed and there was little to stir the village's economy. The cannery was reopened in 1977, however, and now the 55 inhabitants of False Pass share in the fishing boom that has come to the eastern Aleutians.
(Augie Kochuten)

Below
Glaucous-winged gulls gather on the beach at Cape Sarichef on Unimak Island.
(John Sarvis)

Above
Tundra in the Aleutians harbors numerous berry species. This wild strawberry matures in the tundra near Cape Sarichef on Unimak Island.
(John Sarvis)

Dutch Harbor, combined population with Unalaska, 619, viewed from 1,589-foot Mount Ballyhoo, on Unalaska Island. The village of Unalaska, traditionally Aleut, is in the background, across the bay from Dutch Harbor. The expanded fishing economy of the eastern Aleutians centers around Dutch Harbor.
(Bob Nelson, reprinted from *ALASKA*® magazine)

Above
In 1975 Unalaska was not even recorded in the National Marine Fisheries Service count of dollars and pounds landed for U.S. fishing ports. In 1976 the Aleutian community surpassed Kodiak for the number two spot nationally with a crab catch of $48.3 million. In 1978, 14 processors were working at Unalaska and seven more operated at Akutan, giving Unalaska the nation's number one spot. Total production came to about 10 million pounds of crab per week. Here the Ocean Leader *out of Dutch Harbor fights heavy seas while her crew tries to land king crab.*
(Sally Ede Bishop, reprinted from *Fisheries of the North Pacific*)

Right
This underwater photo shows a pod of juvenile king crabs congregated on the sea floor near Unalaska. Podding behavior is thought to be for protection and is seldom seen among adult crabs.
(Bob Nelson)

Left

The village of Saint Paul, population about 500, on the island of Saint Paul in the Pribilofs. The five islands of the Pribilof group—Saint Paul, Saint George, Walrus, Sea Lion Rock and Otter—are about 300 miles off the Alaska mainland in the Bering Sea. Residents of the islands are mostly Aleuts who live in two main villages, Saint Paul and Saint George.
(Susan Hackley Johnson, reprinted from *ALASKA*® magazine)

Below

A blowing snowstorm partially obscures northern fur seals at their rookery on Saint Paul Island.
(Mark Kelley)

Below

In Alaska the red-legged kittiwake, a member of the gull family, breeds only in the Pribilofs and on Buldir and Bogoslof islands in the Aleutians.
(Robert Schulmeister)

Below
*Fumes and vapor rise
from 5,675-foot Mount Cleveland
at the west end of Chuginadak
Island, largest of the Islands of
Four Mountains group.*
(Bob Nelson)

Right
*Nikolski, population 56, clusters
around Nikolski Bay near the
west end of Umnak Island.
Benefits from the burst of fishing
activity farther east have not
reached Nikolski and many men
must still work away from
the village.*
(Lael Morgan, Staff, reprinted from
ALASKA GEOGRAPHIC®)

Left
An arctic fox in its summer pelage on Kiska Island. In winter this species becomes snowy white. Arctic foxes were introduced to many of the islands during the fox-farming era from the 1880's to the 1930's. When fox farming was no longer profitable, the animals were released to fend for themselves. This, in turn, played havoc with other wildlife species, especially ground-nesting birds. Foxes have been eliminated from a few islands to encourage restoration of decimated bird populations.
(R.H. Day)

Left
Among the most feared marine predators are killer whales. This family (the male has the larger dorsal fin) is searching for prey between Agattu and Buldir islands in the western Aleutians.
(John Sarvis)

Right
The Kamchatka rhododendron, which grows to five inches or more, is found at sea level and on alpine meadows of the Aleutians, Kodiak and the Alaska Peninsula.
(R.H. Day)

Below
Twisted metal grids from an abandoned airfield lie partially buried in the sands of Atka Island, one of the Andreanof group of Aleutian Islands.
(Kevin Hekrdle)

Right
The Aleut village of Atka stands about 120 miles northeast of Adak on the shore of Nazan Bay on Atka Island. One of the most isolated communities in Alaska, the village's approximately 92 residents fish for salmon in the fall and halibut and cod year-round.
(Kevin Hekrdle)

Above
Trees are not indigenous to the Aleutians. This small cluster was planted during World War II on Adak Island and is known as Adak National Forest.
(Susan Schulmeister)

Left
Bald eagles are right at home among the craggy cliffs that dominate much of the Aleutian coastline. This eagle was photographed at Adak Island.
(Michael Gordon)

90

Bering Sea Coast

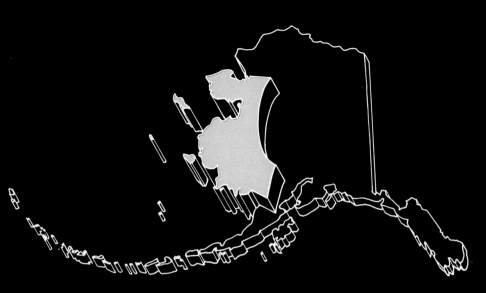

The Bering Sea coast region of Western Alaska, bordered on the north by Kotzebue Sound (an arm of the Chukchi Sea) and on the south by Bristol Bay, extends inland in a convex curve from the Arctic Circle to Telequana Lake, then south to the Katmai National Monument boundary and west to the Kvichak River outlet into Bristol Bay.

Just south of Kotzebue Sound, 200-mile-long Seward Peninsula reaches toward Siberia. The peninsula's tip, Cape Prince of Wales, points seaward to Little Diomede Island, a mere three miles from Big Diomede Island, which is Soviet territory. The Kigluaik, Bendeleben, Darby and other mountains break the terrain of the peninsula's southern half while to the north, the flatlands are etched with countless ponds, lakes, inlets and occasional uplands. The Selawik Hills, summit 3,307 feet, rise in the peninsula's northeast corner.

Norton Sound, a 125-mile arm of the Bering Sea, abuts the Nulato Hills south of the Seward Peninsula. The mighty Yukon River curves around the hills from the east and, with the Kuskokwim River to the south, deposits enough silt to form one of the world's major coastal floodplains, the 200-mile-long and 250-mile-wide Yukon-Kuskokwim Delta.

Even farther south the Kilbuck and Ahklun mountains and the more extensive Kuskokwim Mountains reach the sea at Cape Newenham. This mountainous spine separates the delta from Bristol Bay. The lowland surrounding the bay, intersected by the Nushagak and Kvichak rivers, ties the long tail of the Alaska Peninsula to the rest of Western Alaska.

Offshore, three major island groups rise above the shallow Bering Sea floor. Saint Lawrence is home for more than 800 Siberian Yup'ik Eskimos. Closer to the mainland, across Etolin Strait from the delta, lies Nunivak Island. Saint Matthew Island and smaller Hall Island lie in the central Bering Sea, midway between Saint Lawrence and the Pribilofs.

The northern portion of the Bering Sea coast borders the Arctic and is subject to the severe climate of the Far North. Long, harsh winters with temperatures ranging from -5°F to the low twenties are common. In summer the thermometer reads from the low forties to low sixties. Farther south temperatures moderate a bit. Highs in the thirties to lows around zero are recorded in winter; mid-thirties to mid-sixties are average summer temperatures.

Wind contributes significantly to the region's weather and some areas are seldom without a breeze. North of Bristol Bay rain and snow occur more frequently along the coast than farther inland. Near the bay, however, the opposite is true: precipitation along the coast averages less than farther inland where the highlands are influenced by the moist marine air from Cook Inlet and the Gulf of Alaska.

Transportation along the Bering Sea coast, as in much of Alaska, is by planes and boats in summer, and planes and snow machines in winter. However, there is renewed interest in sled dogs—the Iditarod Trail Sled Dog Race, which begins in Anchorage, crosses the region and terminates in Nome—and higher fuel costs for snow machines may lead to a resurgence of sled dog travel.

Tundra—either wet or upland—characterizes most of the region's vegetation. Grasses, sedges, mosses and lichens and a multitude of wild flowers cover the ground, and scrub willows and alder reach above the tundra. Upriver on the Yukon are stands of white spruce and balsam poplar. Inland on the Kuskokwim River, birch and spruce maintain a tenuous hold in the poor soil. Approaching Bristol Bay the low tundra gives way to thickly forested hillsides . . . some 2.7 million acres in the Bristol Bay area are classified as forest lands.

Although fishing is the backbone of mainly subsistence economy that predominates in the Bering Sea coast region, reindeer are becoming increasingly important. There are about 16,000 animals in 14 herds on the Seward Peninsula, and the village of Stebbins maintains a herd on Stuart Island near the mouth of the Yukon. Additional herds roam Saint Lawrence, Nunivak and Hagemeister islands, as well as the hills around Unalakleet. Support services for herding, such as helicopter rental, and harvesting antlers for processing into medicinal compounds to be sold in the Orient, employ many villagers on a temporary basis and provide substantial cash income for the herds' owners.

Trade center for the Seward Peninsula is Nome (population about 2,900), a booming gold rush town at the turn of the century and today the administrative center for the peninsula. Gold is still an influence in the community, and Alaska Gold Company dredges—considered major attractions by tour companies—are mining the nearby hills.

In the Bering Sea, 130 miles southwest of Nome, is Saint Lawrence Island, whose Eskimo residents follow Siberian Yup'ik ways. Villagers at the island's two communities, Gambell (population 447) and Savoonga (population 409), decided not to participate in the Alaska Native Claims Settlement Act. Instead they chose to keep their 1.2-million-acre reservation and move forward without government cash allotments. Tourism is beginning to play a role in the island's economy and each year increasing numbers of bird enthusiasts visit Saint Lawrence, hoping for a glimpse of Asian species.

The area from Unalakleet north is inhabited mainly by Inupiat Eskimos, who rely mostly on subsistence, although the Bureau of Land Management, Bureau of Indian Affairs and the Public Health Service provide some temporary jobs.

South of Norton Sound and stretching 250 miles to Kuskokwim Bay and inland 200 miles to the Kuskokwim Mountains, is the Yukon-Kuskokwim Delta, a sandy, loamy, fan-shaped area formed mostly by centuries of deposits from the Yukon River. The delta is extremely fertile and supports abundant plant

INDEX TO
BERING SEA COAST
GEOGRAPHIC FEATURES

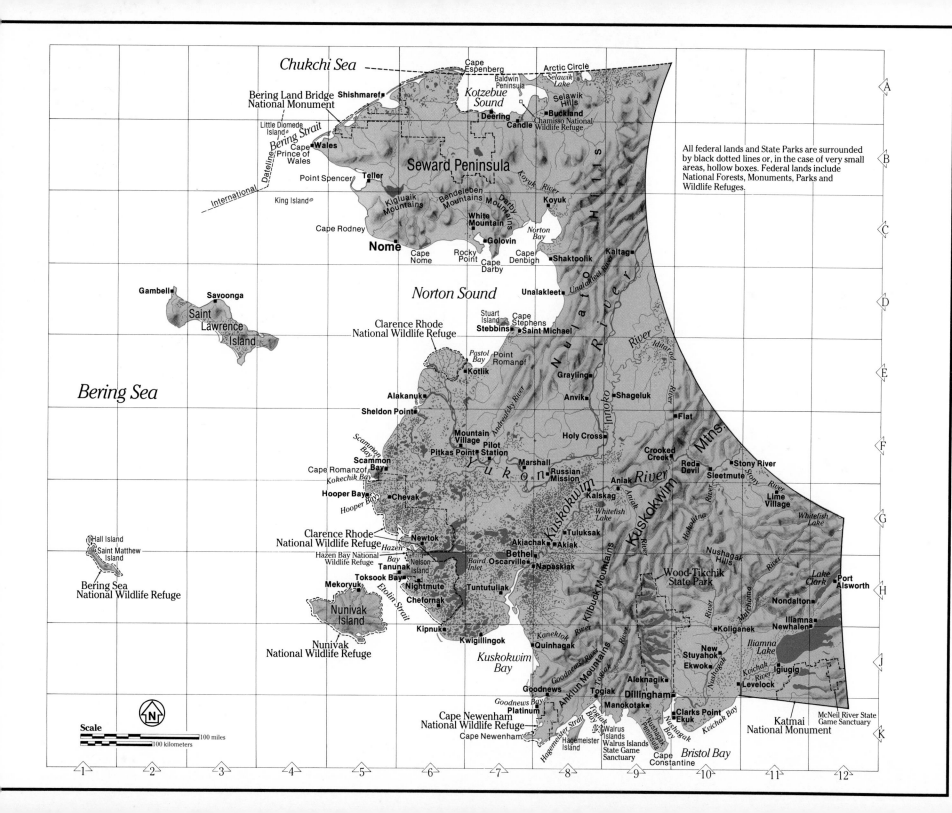

Chukchi Sea

Cape Espenberg

Arctic Circle

Baldwin Peninsula

Selawik Lake

Bering Land Bridge National Monument

Shishmaref

Kotzebue Sound

Selawik Hills

Deering

Buckland

Candle

Chamisso National Wildlife Refuge

Little Diomede Island

Cape **Wales** Prince of Wales

Bering Strait

Seward Peninsula

Darby

Koyuk River

Dateline

Point Spencer **Teller**

International

King Island

Kigluaik Mountains

Bendeleben Mountains

Darby Mountains

Koyuk

Nulato Hills

Cape Rodney

White Mountain

Norton Bay

Golovin

Nome

Cape Nome

Rocky Point

Cape Darby

Cape Denbigh

Shaktoolik

Kaltag

Norton Sound

Unalakleet

Unalakleet River

Stuart Island

Cape Stephens

Clarence Rhode National Wildlife Refuge

Stebbins

Saint Michael

Bering Sea

Gambell

Savoonga

Saint Lawrence Island

Pastol Bay

Point Romanof

Kotlik

Idatarod

River

Grayling

Anvik

Shageluk

Innoko River

Innoko

Alakanuk

Andreafsky River

Sheldon Point

Holy Cross

Flat

Crooked Creek

Mtns.

Mountain Village

Pitkas Point

Pilot Station

Marshall

Scammon Bay

Scammon Bay

Yukon

Russian Mission

Red **Devil**

Stony River

Cape Romanzof

Kokechik Bay

Aniak

Kuskokwim

Aniak River

Stony River

Sleetmute

Lime Village

Hooper Bay

Chevak

Whitefish Lake

Whitefish Lake

Hooper Bay

Kuskokwim River

Tuluksak

Kuskokwim

Hall Island

Saint Matthew Island

Clarence Rhode National Wildlife Refuge

Hazen Bay National Wildlife Refuge

Hazen Bay

Newtok

Akiachak

Akiak

Hoholitna River

Mulchatna River

Bering Sea National Wildlife Refuge

Tanunak

Nelson Island

Baird Inlet

Bethel

Oscarville

Napaskiak

Kilbuck Mountains

Nushagak Hills

Lake Clark

Port Alsworth

Toksook Bay

Mekoryuk

Nightmute

Tuntutuliak

Etolin Strait

Chefornak

Wood-Tikchik State Park

Nondalton

Nunivak Island

Illamna

Newhalen

Kipnuk

Nunivak National Wildlife Refuge

Kanektok River

Koliganek

Iliamna Lake

Kwigillingok

Quinhagak

Goodnews River

Ahklun Mountains

Togiak River

Nushagak River

New **Stuyahok**

Ekwok

Igiugig

Kvichak River

Levelock

Kuskokwim Bay

Goodnews

Goodnews Bay

Platinum

Cape Newenham National Wildlife Refuge

Cape Newenham

Togiak Bay

Hagemeister Strait

Hagemeister Island

Togiak Peninsula

Togiak

Manokotak

Aleknagik

Dillingham

Nushagak Bay

Kvichak Bay

Clarks Point

Ekuk

Cape Constantine

Katmai National Monument

McNeil River State Game Sanctuary

Walrus Islands

Walrus Islands State Game Sanctuary

Bristol Bay

Scale

100 miles

100 kilometers

N

A B C D E F G H J K

1 2 3 4 5 6 7 8 9 10 11 12

and animal life. The Delta is also wet—not only do the Yukon and Kuskokwim rivers meander across this broad plain, but there are innumerable streams, sloughs, ponds and lakes, in addition to vast tidal flats. Most of the more than 100 villages that dot the delta are Yup'ik Eskimo, although some farther inland are Athabascan Indian.

Bethel, heart of the Delta and Western Alaska's largest community (population 3,600), serves as the commercial and administrative headquarters. Goods and passengers are flown or barged to Bethel, then transshipped to the villages on bush planes, small barges and shallow-draft boats.

Subsistence, supplemented by dollars from commercial fishing for salmon, is the way of life for most delta residents. Salmon is caught in the summer, and dried and stored for winter. In winter, residents fish through the ice for burbot, sheefish, whitefish, pike and blackfish. Subsistence hunters harvest game, including ptarmigan, snowshoe hare, beaver, moose and caribou, in addition to substantial numbers of geese, ducks and lesser sandhill cranes, plus some seals, walrus, sea lions and beluga whales.

South and east of Kuskokwim Bay and around the corner from Cape Newenham is Bristol Bay, where the economy has traditionally been based on the sea—primarily the salmon industry, although the smaller populations of sheefish and whitefish are significant. Streams and rivers flowing into the bay nourish the largest red salmon spawning grounds in the world, and in 1979 the total run was 40 million fish. Of the total 1979 red salmon catch of 28,360,000 fish, 21,429,000 came from Bristol Bay.

The Nushagak River system produces the area's major pink salmon run and biologists forecast a record return for 1980. Supplies for this fishery, as well as for those destined for most of the villages, funnel through Dillingham (population 1,360), at the confluence of the Wood and Nushagak rivers. Dillingham is also the major center for fish processing in the bay area.

Above
Bull walrus gather under a pinnacle at a point on Round Island. The island is the only known hauling-out spot used exclusively by breeding bulls.
(Brian Milne, reprinted from *ALASKA*® magazine)

Opposite
Wales, population about 150, is at the western tip of the Seward Peninsula. Once one of the largest Inupiat Eskimo villages, residents of Wales today rely on fishing, hunting, reindeer herding and temporary work with various government agencies.
(Mark McDermott)

Left
During summer many Nome residents move to fish camp to catch and dry this staple of the northern diet. Salmon enter several rivers, both east and west of Nome, on the way to spawning streams.
(Jerrianne Lowther, Staff)

Above
Jason Harold, with an expression discouraging all intruders, clears away the ice from his fishing hole in a slough near Unalakleet.
(Jim Simmen)

Right
Henry Oyoumick picks Dolly Varden from a net strung underneath the ice of the Unalakleet River.
(Jim Greenough)

101

Below
Fourteen reindeer herds with more than 16,000 animals graze on the Seward Peninsula and eastern Norton Sound. The antlers are sold in the Orient for medicinal purposes and the meat and hides from the winter butchering are consumed locally. This herd grazes near Candle not far from the northern coast of the peninsula.
(George Herben)

Right
Corraled reindeer wait their turn to have their antlers clipped at Nome. Selling of antlers brings thousands of dollars into the villages.
(Mark Rauzon)

Far right
Nome, population about 2,900, serves as the commercial center for the Seward Peninsula. Saloons, gift shops, cafes, a drug store, appliance store, grocery stores and Alaska Commercial Company department store line Nome's main street.
(Penny Rennick, Staff)

Top
A "grizzly" shakes larger rocks from the dirt at this gold mine near the Casadepaga River northeast of Nome. A sluice box attached to the grizzly separates the heavier gold from the gravel. Getting heavy equipment to an isolated mine can be a challenge. This equipment arrived at Nome by barge, and then was trucked to the mine 70 miles away.
(Harry Walker)

Above
Numerous dredges—both working and abandoned—are stationed in the hills around Nome. At the turn of the century Nome was booming. Later the community languished for many years because the price of gold was not high enough to allow profitable extraction. Now, however, the dredges of Alaska Gold Company are once again mining the rich deposits still abundant in the area.
(Penny Rennick, Staff)

Above
Some areas of the Bering Sea coast are swept almost constantly by winds. These hardy residents of Toksook Bay, population 336, on the Yukon-Kuskokwim Delta must brave the elements just to move around their village.
(John McDonald)

Left
The mail plane, lifeline of bush Alaska, carries not only the mail but also visitors, supplies, equipment and special surprises such as Christmas presents. These villagers gather around a mail plane waiting at Toksook Bay.
(John McDonald)

Left
Photographer Harry Walker commemorated the last morning of his trip down the Yukon by taking this photo of his canoe tied to a piece of driftwood stuck into the mud of the Yukon-Kuskokwim Delta between Mountain Village and Alakanuk.

Below
Meandering rivers and a multitude of lakes characterize the Yukon-Kuskokwim Delta, 2,800 square miles of which is included in the Clarence Rhode National Wildlife Refuge.
(Jerry L. Hout, reprinted from
ALASKA GEOGRAPHIC®)

Left
The fresh waters around Bristol Bay nourish the largest red salmon population in the world. In 1979, 40 million fish returned to the area to spawn.
(Steve McCutcheon)

Right
Mrs. Simeon Bartman of Manokotak sets aside the pinkish-orange roe as she cleans salmon on this Bristol Bay beach.
(Lael Morgan, Staff, reprinted from *ALASKA GEOGRAPHIC*®)

Arctic

The Arctic is separated from the rest of Alaska by an invisible line that runs west along the crest of the Brooks Range to Mount Igikpak, near the head of the Noatak River, then curves south past the village of Kobuk to the Arctic Circle and extends west to reach the Chukchi Sea just south of Kotzebue.

The Brooks Range is named for Alfred Brooks (1871-1924), chief Alaskan geologist for the U.S. Geological Survey for more than 20 years. Length of the range from the Canadian border to the Chukchi Sea is 600 line-of-sight miles; however, a measurement of the crest of the range as it twists and turns across the state is 720 miles. The Brooks Range rises in Yukon Territory in the Barn Mountains, the British Mountains and the Buckland Hills. In Alaska, and from east to west, the range encompasses the Davidson Mountains, Romanzof Mountains—the highest and widest portion of the range—the Sadlerochit and Shublik mountains, Philip Smith and Endicott mountains. The Schwatka group,

which harbors the Arrigetch Peaks and Mount Igikpak, merge with the Baird and De Long mountains at the western end of the range.

Gently sloping foothills slip from the mountain peaks to the arctic coastal plain. These are essentially rocky slopes cut by rivers which flow to broad deltas along the coast. The Colville River, largest drainage system in the Arctic, joins with the Canning, Sagavanirktok and numerous other rivers to carry rain and snow-melt northward. The Noatak and Kobuk drain the Arctic's western and southwestern reaches.

Steady, strong winds, cold temperatures and low precipitation characterize the arctic climate zone. The Beaufort and Chukchi seas moderate the climate somewhat but temperatures at Barrow, near the northernmost extension of North America, average between 30°F and 40°F in July and August and between -15°F and -18°F in January and February. Temperature inversions are common throughout the Arctic. The cooling trend of rising air masses is reversed by atmos-

Left

A rainbow shimmers above the tundra decked in late fall colors in the Anaktuvuk River valley. The river flows north from the Brooks Range to the Colville River in the central Arctic.
(George Wuerthner)

Right

Its crucial importance as the summer breeding ground for the Porcupine caribou herd was a major factor in setting aside the lands of the William O. Douglas Arctic Wildlife Range. The annual migration route takes the herd from the North Slope across the Brooks Range to the Ogilvie Mountains and Peel River country of Yukon Territory.
(Steve McCutcheon)

pheric conditions and colder air is trapped near the ground. If air pollution is present under these conditions, its effect is accentuated.

Permafrost, beginning just a few inches under the surface and extending down to 2,000 feet, underlies most of the Arctic. Tundra and bog soils are most common because permafrost impedes drainage. Disturbing the plant cover brings about thawing of the permafrost which, in turn, leads to erosion. Soil erosion along tracked vehicle routes in the Arctic was found to be particularly damaging, so travel is restricted to winter or vehicles are equipped with giant, low-pressure tires which have little or no effect on the landscape.

The region's vegetation consists of several varieties of tundra. Higher elevations support alpine tundra:

lichens, grasses, sedges, some herbs such as mountain avens and saxifrage. Moss campion grows on drier talus slopes. Cottongrass, mosses, lichens, dwarf birch and willows cover the foothills. Sedges, mosses, cottongrass and lousewort predominate on the boggy plain, and high brush vegetation, typified by willow and alder, grows along major river flood plains.

While many square miles are required to sustain large mammals in the Arctic, numerous species including moose, wolves, brown/grizzly bears, and Dall sheep—do make their homes on the northern tundra. Caribou, grouped into two major herds—Western Arctic and Porcupine—roam all but the rockiest slopes of the Brooks Range. Smaller mammals—wolverines, weasels, a few river otters, snowshoe hares, lynx, shrews, lemmings and voles—also live in the Arctic. On the coastal plain the ranges of the arctic fox and red fox overlap. After being hunted out of the region, musk ox have been reintroduced and herds are now doing well near coastal river valleys. Many bird species come to the Arctic to breed and raise their young, although few species overwinter.

Several key wildlife habitats have been set aside as national monuments and wildlife refuges. The William O. Douglas Arctic Wildlife Range, crucial to the survival of the Porcupine caribou herd, is perhaps the most notable; but others such as Noatak, Cape Krusenstern, Kobuk Valley and Selawik were created for the protection of specific geological phenomena and wildlife species.

The frigid waters of the Beaufort and Chukchi seas support populations of polar bears, walrus, bowhead and beluga whales, and bearded and ringed seals. In the short summer months when the ice retreats from the coast, harbor seals, harbor porpoises, and killer and gray whales pass by. Rarer species of great whales—the fin, sei, and little piked—also have been reported in Chukchi waters.

Transportation in the Arctic is chiefly by boat and small plane in summer and by plane and snow machine in winter. Dog teams used to be a major means of moving goods and people but the advent of snow machines brought about their decline. Lately, however, rising fuel costs and mechanical unreliability have led to a resurgence of dog team travel. Once a year a fleet of tug-pulled barges from the Lower 48 brings supplies and equipment to coastal villages and the oil-drilling operations at Prudhoe.

Few settlements have been established in the Arctic. Barrow (population about 2,700) serves as the trade center for the North Slope Borough where seven smaller villages—Wainwright, Point Lay, Point Hope, Atkasook, Nuiqsut, Anaktuvuk Pass, Kaktovik—and the oil complex at Prudhoe Bay are located. Commerce among the 10 or so villages in the southwestern Arctic revolves around Kotzebue (population 2,500). From Kotzebue supplies are shipped to

Below
Polygonal forms created by the interaction of vegetation, soil, and the expansion and contraction of the shallow layer of earth above the permafrost characterize much of the North Slope's tundra.
(Steve McCutcheon)

Opposite
Ice wedges thrust out from surrounding permafrost form pingos, the only significant natural elevations on the coastal plain north of the Brooks Range.
(Steve McCutcheon)

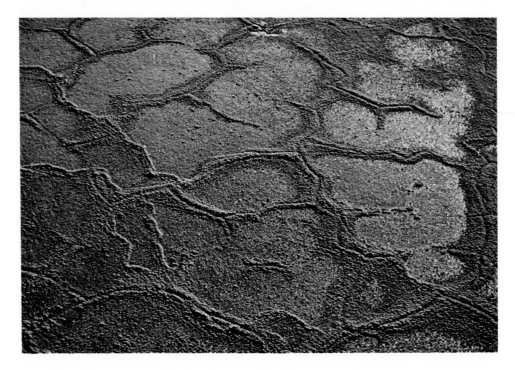

Kobuk, Shungnak, Ambler, Kiana and Noorvik in the Kobuk River valley; Noatak in the Noatak River valley; Kivalina along the coast; Selawik; and other smaller villages.

Oil and subsistence provide the majority of economic support for the Arctic. From discovery of the oil fields near Prudhoe Bay in 1968, production levels, in late 1979, allowed shipment of 1.2 million barrels of oil per day through the trans-Alaska pipeline to Valdez, 800 miles to the south. Development of the oil fields and related construction created jobs for many arctic residents and has provided the economic stimulus for new houses, schools, hospitals and civic buildings.

Residents of the smaller villages rely on subsistence and temporary work, usually in construction or government projects. Caribou are important to inland Eskimos, while coastal villagers depend on fish and marine mammals, such as bearded seals, walrus and beluga whales.

Oil does not dominate the economy of Kotzebue and its trading region as it does farther north. Commercial fishing, trapping, fur buying and tourism generate income for this part of the Arctic. NANA, the Native regional corporation for Northwestern Alaska, oversees the largest reindeer herd in Alaska, marketing the antlers in the Orient and selling the meat locally. The NANA-operated Museum of the Arctic contains a jade manufacturing operation, displays and demonstrations of Native crafts and skills, and a diorama of Alaska wildlife. The community college at Kotzebue, part of the University of Alaska, is experimenting with alternative energy sources including wind power. Since 1977 Inupiat from surrounding villages have tended gardens under a special project to determine if vegetables and flowers can be grown successfully, and perhaps even profitably. Twenty plots in the village of Ambler produced crops in 1977. In 1979 more than 500 plots in the Kotzebue region and south in the Nome area were under cultivation.

INDEX TO ARCTIC GEOGRAPHIC FEATURES

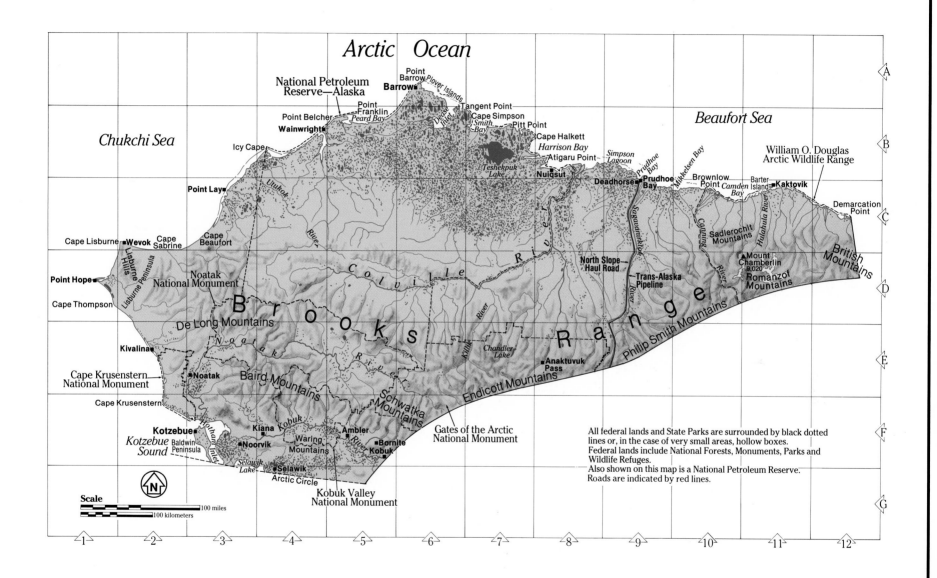

Arctic Ocean

Chukchi Sea

Beaufort Sea

National Petroleum
Reserve—Alaska

Point
Barrow *Plover Islands*
Barrow

Point
Franklin
Point Belcher *Peard Bay*
Wainwright

Tangent Point
Cape Simpson
*Smith
Bay* Pitt Point

Cape Halkett
Harrison Bay
Atigaru Point

*Simpson
Lagoon*

William O. Douglas
Arctic Wildlife Range

Icy Cape

*Dease
Inlet*

*Teshekpuk
Lake*

Mikkelsen Bay

Nuiqsut

*Prudhoe
Bay*

Brownlow
Point *Camden
Bay*
Barter
Island **Kaktovik**

Deadhorse **Prudhoe
Bay**

Demarcation
Point

Point Lay

Utukok

River

North Slope—
Haul Road

Trans-Alaska
Pipeline

Sagavanirktok

Conning

Sadlerochit
Mountains

Hulahula River

**British
Mountains**

Cape Lisburne **Wevok** Cape
Sabrine

Cape
Beaufort

C o l v i l l e   R i v e r

▲Mount
Chamberlin
9,020

*Romanzof
Mountains*

Point Hope

Lisburne Peninsula *Lisburne
Hills*

Noatak
National Monument

B r o o k s   R a n g e

River

Cape Thompson

De Long Mountains

*Killik
River*

*Chandler
Lake*

Philip Smith Mountains

N o a t a k

Kivalina

River

Endicott Mountains

Cape Krusenstern
National Monument

Noatak

Baird Mountains

Schwatka
Mountains

**Anaktuvuk
Pass**

Cape Krusenstern

Kobuk

Kiana

Ambler

Bornite

Gates of the Arctic
National Monument

Kotzebue

Hotham Inlet

Waring
Mountains

River

Kobuk

*Kotzebue
Sound*

Baldwin
Peninsula

Noorvik

All federal lands and State Parks are surrounded by black dotted
lines or, in the case of very small areas, hollow boxes.
Federal lands include National Forests, Monuments, Parks and
Wildlife Refuges.
Also shown on this map is a National Petroleum Reserve.
Roads are indicated by red lines.

*Selawik
Lake*

Selawik

Arctic Circle

Kobuk Valley
National Monument

Scale

100 miles

100 kilometers

N

A
B
C
D
E
F
G

1   2   3   4   5   6   7   8   9   10   11   12

Left
The sheer, snow-covered slopes of the Brooks Range where it crosses the southern portion of the William O. Douglas Arctic Wildlife Range.
(Dennis and Debbie Miller)

Right
Light reflects off the braided Hulahula River in the William O. Douglas Arctic Wildlife Range.
(Dennis and Debbie Miller)

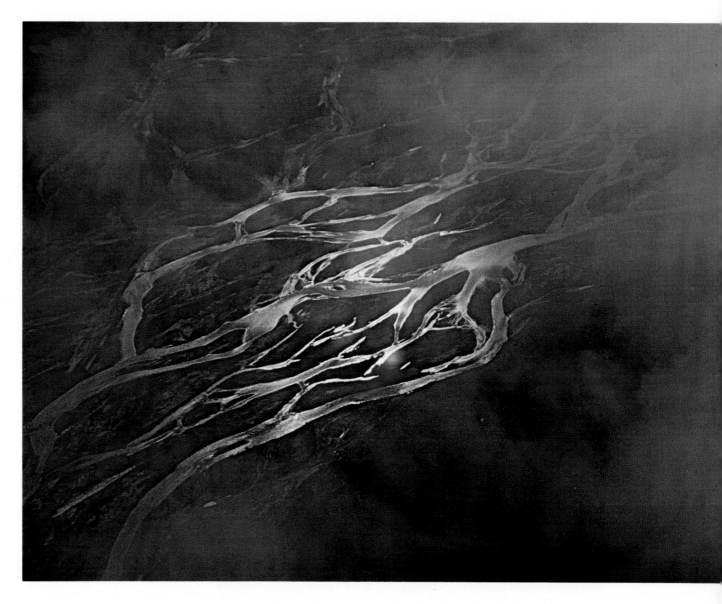

Above
Duck Island, a man-made island near Prudhoe Bay, on which Exxon has built a drilling rig.
(George Herben)

Left
Wildlife abounds on the waterways and tundra of the North Slope. Many species, such as this arctic loon family at Prudhoe Bay, will migrate out of the area in late summer to winter in more moderate climates.
(George Herben)

Right
The British Petroleum-Sohio facilities at Prudhoe Bay. BP-Sohio and Atlantic Richfield are the two major operators of the Prudhoe Bay complex.
(George Herben)

Left

Aerial view of Barrow, headquarters of the North Slope Borough and the commercial center of Alaska north of the Brooks Range. The airport, which serves Wien Air Alaska and several smaller charter services, extends diagonally across the top of the photo. The Top of the World Hotel is the inverted L-shaped building with the long pipe reaching to the surf. The three large buildings in the lower left are: North Slope Borough headquarters (blue roof); the store owned by the village corporation; and the Arctic Slope Regional Corporation headquarters (with orange stairway covering).
(Penny Rennick, Staff, reprinted from *ALASKA®* magazine)

Inupiat Eskimo whalers at Point Barrow search the ice leads (areas of open water which form when breakup comes) for signs of migrating bowheads.
(Alan Crane, reprinted from *ALASKA®* magazine)

Top
Frame for Ole and Manya Wik's semi-underground sod house in the Kobuk valley. The completed frame will be covered with plastic sheeting and moss, then backfilled with dirt. Additional insulation will be provided by snow.
(Manya Wik)

Above
Ole Wik takes the bedding out to air beside his semi-underground sod house.
(Manya Wik)

Above
On a foggy morning in the Kobuk valley, Keith Jones of Ambler hauls two sleds and a kayak by dog team to spring camp.
(Manya Wik)

Right
Eskimo women at Kobuk clean and hang fish on racks to dry. Fish is a staple in the diet of the Inupiat of the southwestern Arctic.
(William Sherwonit)

Below
Fishermen gather to sell their chum salmon to a buyer at Kotzebue, site of the farthest north commercial fishery.
(Bruce Baker, reprinted from *ALASKA*® magazine)

Right
NANA, the Native regional corporation for the Kotzebue area, manages the largest reindeer herd in Alaska. About 3,575 animals graze on the Baldwin Peninsula (on which Kotzebue is situated) and on the NANA allotment on the north coast of the Seward Peninsula. In 1979 the corporation was awarded a second grazing plot on the peninsula. In addition, NANA manages a little over 3,000 animals on the Hadley allotment at the eastern end of the Seward Peninsula. During the summer the antlers are cut from the reindeer and sold to processors who grind the antlers into a compound for resale in the Orient.
(George Herben)

The changing seasons at Kotzebue: July (below) and March (right). In summer commerce, tourism, commercial fishing and subsistence support the town's 2,526 residents. In winter trapping becomes a source of revenue. Kotzebue boasts a radio station, two fine museums and a community college.
(Both by George Herben)

126

Appendix

Portions of the following are excerpted from *The MILEPOST®* (1980 edition) available for $7.95 (plus $1.00 fourth class or $2.75 first class postage and handling), and *THE ALASKA ALMANAC®* (1980 edition) available for $3.95 (plus $.75 postage and handling); both from Alaska Northwest Publishing Company, Box 4-EEE, Anchorage, Alaska 99509.

OPPOSITE: Alaska's plants and wildlife, painted by the late Bill Berry, one of Alaska's leading artists for many years. The 26½-inch by 40-inch map, detailing 120 flowers, animals, fishes and birds, is available for $6.00 (plus $.50 postage and handling) from Alaska Northwest Publishing, Box 4-EEE, Anchorage, Alaska 99509. Maps come in a protective tube and with a numbered key identifying each species.

PHYSICAL GEOGRAPHY OF ALASKA

THE LAND

At first glance it seems impossible that such a huge country as Alaska has not been settled. Thousands of acres of forest and tundra, miles and miles of rivers and streams, hidden valleys, bays, coves and mountains, are spread across an area so vast that it staggers the imagination. Yet, over two-thirds of the population of Alaska remains clustered around two major centers of commerce and survival. Compared to the settlement of the West, Alaska is not settled at all.

Visitors flying over the state are always impressed by the immense areas with no sign of humanity. Current assessments indicate that approximately 160,000 acres of Alaska have been cleared, built on or otherwise directly altered by man, either by settlement or resource development, including mining, pipeline construction, and agriculture. In comparison to the 375 million acres of land which constitute the total of the state, the settled or altered area currently amounts to less than 1/20th of a percent.

There are significant reasons for this lack of development in Alaska. Frozen for long periods in the dark of the Arctic, much of the land cannot support quantities of people or industry and where the winters are "warm," the mountains, glaciers, rivers and oceans prevent easy access for commerce and trade.

The status of land, especially in Alaska, is constantly changing. In most places, the free market affects patterns of land ownership, but in Alaska, all land ownership patterns until recently were the result of a century-long process of a single landowner, the United States government.

The Statehood Act, signed into law in 1958, brought about the beginning of a dramatic shift in land ownership patterns. It authorized the state to select a total of 103.35 million of the 375 million acres of land and inland waters in Alaska. Under the Submerged Lands Act, the state also has title to submerged lands under navigable inland waters. In passing the Statehood Act, Congress cited economic independence and the need to open Alaska to economic development as the primary purposes for large Alaska land grants.

The issue of the Native claims in Alaska was cleared with the passage of the Alaska Native Claims Settlement Act (ANCSA) on December 18, 1971. This Act of Congress, provided for creation of Alaska Native village and regional corporations, and gave the Alaska Eskimos, Aleuts and Indians nearly one billion dollars and the right to select 44 million acres from a land "pool" of some 116 million acres.

Immediately after the passage of the Settlement Act, the state filed for the selection of some 77 million acres of land before the creation of some Native withdrawals and with-

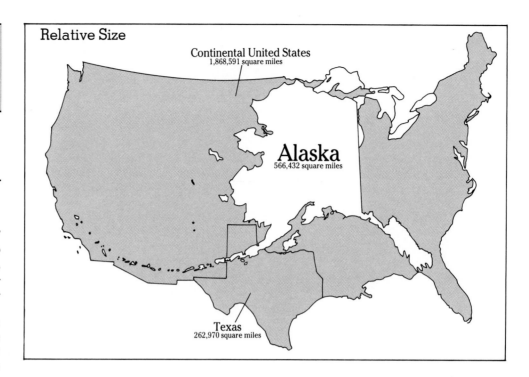

Relative Size

Continental United States
1,868,591 square miles

Alaska
566,432 square miles

Texas
262,970 square miles

drawals for study as "National Interest Lands." The Department of the Interior refused to recognize these selections. In September 1972, the litigation initiated by the state was resolved by a settlement affirming state selection of 41 million acres.

Section 17 of the Settlement Act, in addition to establishing a Joint Federal-State Land Use Planning Commission, directed the Secretary of the Interior to withdraw from public use up to 80 million acres of land in Alaska for study as possible national parks, wildlife refuges, forests and wild and scenic rivers. These were the "National Interest Lands" Congress was to decide upon as set forth in Section 17(d) (2) of the Settlement Act, by December 18, 1978. The U.S. House of Representatives passed a Bill (HR-39) which would have designated 124 million acres of national parks, forests and wildlife refuges, and designated millions of acres of these and existing parks, forests and refuges as wilderness. Although a bill was reported out of Committee, it failed to pass the Senate before Congress adjourned.

In November 1978, the Secretary of the Interior published a draft environmental impact supplement which listed the options that the executive branch of the federal government could take to protect federal lands in Alaska until the 96th Congress could consider the creation of new parks, wildlife refuges, wild and scenic rivers and forests. In keeping with this objective, the Secretary of the Interior withdrew from most public uses, about 114 million acres of land in Alaska, under provisions of the 1976 Federal Land Policy and Management Act. On December 1, 1978, the President, under the authority of the 1906 Antiquities Act, designated 56 million acres of these lands as National Monuments.

Alaska's land will continue to be a controversial and complex subject for some time. Resolution of the D-2 issue, distribution of land to the Native village and regional corporations, the State of Alaska, and private citizens in the state, will require time. Numerous land issues, created by large land exchanges, conflicting land use and management policies, and overlapping resources will require constant cooperation between landowners if the issues are going to be solved successfully.

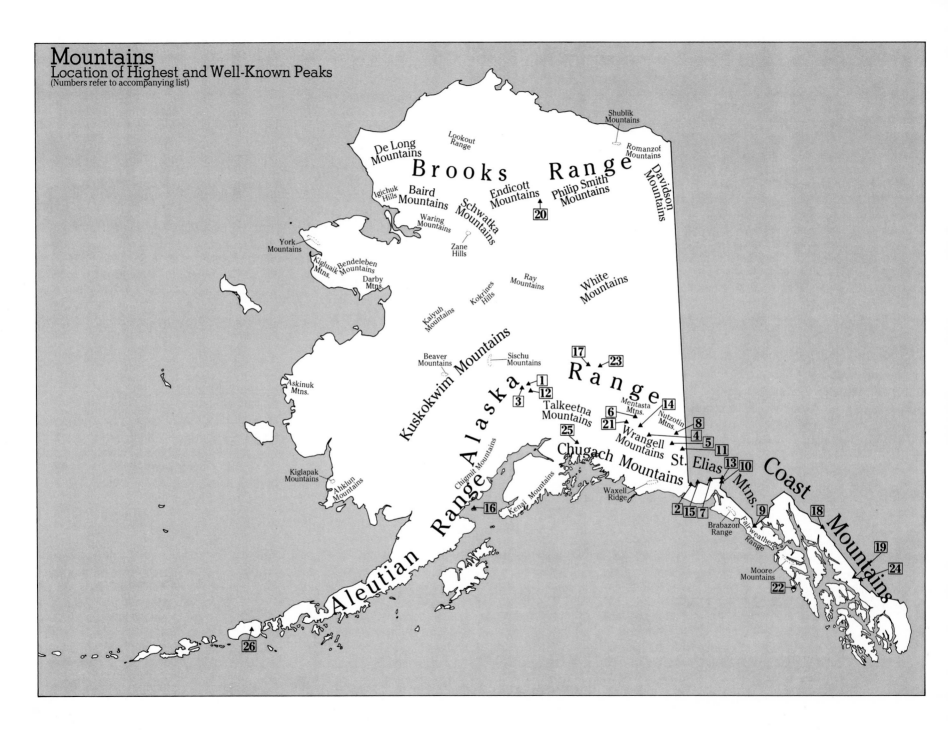

Mountains
Location of Highest and Well-Known Peaks
(Numbers refer to accompanying list)

Shublik Mountains

Lookout Range

De Long Mountains

Romanzof Mountains

Davidson Mountains

Brooks   Range

Igichuk Hills

Baird Mountains

Endicott Mountains

Philip Smith Mountains

20

Schwatka Mountains

Waring Mountains

Zane Hills

York Mountains

Kigluaik Mtns.

Bendeleben Mountains

Darby Mtns.

Ray Mountains

White Mountains

Katyuh Mountains

Kokrines Hills

Beaver Mountains

Sischu Mountains

17   23

Kuskokwim Mountains

1   12

3

Range

Mentasta Mtns.

14

Talkeetna Mountains

6

Nutzotin Mtns.

Alaska

21

8

25

4   5

Wrangell Mountains

11

Chugach Mountains

St. Elias

13   10

Coast

Askinuk Mtns.

Chigmit Mountains

Waxell Ridge

Mtns.

18

Kiglapak Mountains

Ahklun Mountains

Kenai Mountains

2   15   7

9

19

Aleutian   Range

16

Brabazon Range

Fairweather Range

Moore Mountains

24

22

26

Mountains

132

MOUNTAINS

Of the 20 highest mountains in the United States, 17 are in Alaska, which has 19 peaks over 14,000 feet. The U.S. Geological Survey lists them as follows:

Highest Mountains

	ELEVATION
McKinley, South Peak* (1)	20,320
McKinley, North Peak* (1)	19,470
Saint Elias** (2)	18,008
Foraker (3)	17,400
Blackburn (4)	16,523
Bona (5)	16,421
Sanford (6)	16,237
South Buttress (1)	15,885
Vancouver** (7)	15,700
Churchill (8)	15,638
Fairweather** (9)	15,300

	ELEVATION
Hubbard** (10)	15,015
Bear (11)	14,831
East Buttress (1)	14,730
Hunter (12)	14,573
Alverstone** (13)	14,565
Browne Tower (1)	14,530
Wrangell (14)	14,163
Augusta** (15)	14,070

* The two peaks of Mount McKinley are known collectively as the Churchill Peaks.
** On Alaska-Canada border.

Other Well-Known Alaska Mountains

	ELEVATION
Augustine Volcano (16)	4,025
Deborah (17)	12,339
Devils Paw (18)	8,584
Devils Thumb (19)	9,077
Doonerak (20)	7,610
Drum (21)	12,010
Edgecumbe (22)	3,201
Hayes (23)	13,832
Kates Needle (24)	10,002
Marcus Baker (25)	13,176
Shishaldin (26)	9,372

Mountain Ranges

	ELEVATION		ELEVATION		ELEVATION
Ahklun Mountains	1,000-3,000	De Long Mountains	to 4,886	Ray Mountains	2,500-5,500
Alaska Range	to 20,320	Endicott Mountains	to 7,000	Romanzof Mountains	to 8,700
Aleutian Range	to 7,585	Fairweather Range	to 15,300	Saint Elias Mountains	to 18,000
Askinuk Mountains	to 2,342	Igichuk Hills	to 2,000	Schwatka Mountains	to 8,800
Baird Mountains	to 4,300	Kaiyuh Mountains	1,000-2,844	Shublik Mountains	to 4,500
Bendeleben Mountains	to 3,730	Kenai Mountains	to 6,000	Sischu Mountains	to 2,422
Brabazon Range	to 5,515	Kiglapak Mountains	to 1,070	Talkeetna Mountains	6,000-8,800
Brooks Range	4,000-9,000	Kigluaik Mountains	to 4,714	Waring Mountains	to 1,800
Chigmit Mountains	to 5,000	Kuskokwim Mountains	to 3,973	Waxell Ridge	4,000-10,000
Chugach Mountains	to 13,176	Lookout Range	to 2,400	White Mountains	to 5,000
Coast Mountains	to 18,000	Mentasta Mountains	4,000-7,000	Wrangell Mountains	to 16,421
Darby Mountains	to 3,083	Moore Mountains	to 3,000	York Mountains	to 2,349
Davidson Mountains	to 5,540	Nutzotin Mountains	5,000-8,000	Zane Hills	to 4,053

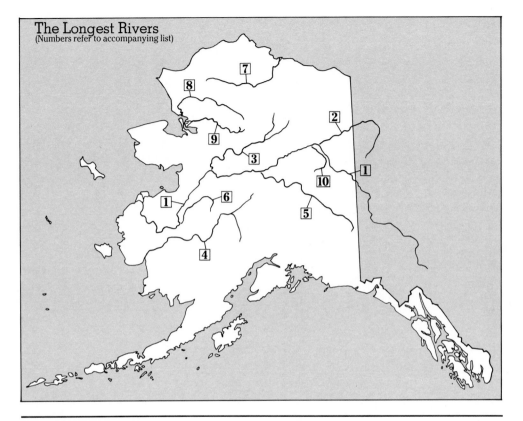

The Longest Rivers
(Numbers refer to accompanying list)

LAKES

There are 94 lakes with surface areas of more than 10 square miles among Alaska's more than 3 million lakes. According to a 1963 report of the U.S. Geological Survey, the 10 largest (larger than 20 acres) natural fresh-water lakes are:

	SQUARE MILES
Iliamna	1,000
Becharof	458
Teshekpuk	315
Naknek	242
Tustumena	117
Clark	110
Dall	100
Upper Ugashik	75
Lower Ugashik	72
Kukaklek	72

ISLANDS

Southeastern Alaska contains about 1,000 of the state's 1,800 named islands, rocks and reefs; several thousand remain unnamed. The state's 10 largest islands, according to U.S. Geological Survey and Bureau of Land Management figures, are:

	SQUARE MILES
Kodiak	3,588
Prince of Wales	2,231
Chichagof	2,062
Saint Lawrence	1,780*
Admiralty	1,709
Baranof	1,636
Nunivak	1,600*
Unimak	1,600
Revillagigedo	1,134
Kupreanof	1,084

* Estimate

RIVERS

Following are the 10 longest rivers in Alaska, as provided to the Joint Federal-State Land Use Planning Commission by the Army Corps of Engineers (see map above):

	MILES
Yukon (1)	1,875
Porcupine (2)	555
Koyukuk (3)	554
Kuskokwim (4)	540
Tanana (5)	531
Innoko (6)	463
Colville (7)	428
Noatak (8)	396
Kobuk (9)	347
Birch Creek (10)	314

The Yukon flows about 1,400 miles in Alaska; the remainder is in Canada. It ranks fourth in North America in length, fifth in drainage area (327,600 square miles). About two-thirds of the Porcupine's length is in Canada.

GLACIERS AND ICE FIELDS

Ice fields cover 28,800 square miles—4.9%—of Alaska. The greatest concentrations are in the Alaska Range, the Wrangell Mountains and the coastal system of the Coast, Saint Elias, Chugach and Kenai mountains, where annual precipitation is high (see map, right).

Alaska's well-known glaciers all fall within these massive ice fields (see below). Information provided by the U.S. Geological Survey shows the area of most extensive ice coverage to be:

Major Ice Fields
(Numbers refer to accompanying list)

Area shown in detail

	SQUARE MILES
Chugach Mountains, Bering Glacier and Bagley Icefield area (1)	4,681
Chugach Mountains, central and western areas (2) (Columbia, Matanuska, Worthington and Valdez glaciers)	3,539
Wrangell Mountains (3)	3,228
Saint Elias Mountains (4) (Malaspina and Hubbard glaciers)	2,937
Glacier Bay National Monument area (5)	2,574
Kenai Mountains (6) (Harding Icefield, Portage Glacier)	1,856
Alaska Range, southwestern area (7)	1,844
Alaska Range, Mount McKinley area (8) (Muldrow, Ruth, Tokositna, Kahiltna and Eldridge glaciers)	1,731
Alaska Range, east of George Parks Highway (9)	1,451
Stikine Icefield (10)	1,301
Juneau Icefield (11) (Mendenhall and Taku glaciers)	1,216
TOTAL	26,358

Worthington (Richardson Highway), Matanuska (Glenn Highway), Portage (Anchorage-Seward Highway) and Mendenhall (a few miles from Juneau) are Alaska's better-known glaciers accessible by road. In addition, Sheridan Glacier may be reached by a short drive from Cordova. Valdez Glacier is only a few miles from the town of Valdez. The sediment-covered terminus of Muldrow Glacier in Mount McKinley National Park is visible at a distance for several miles along the park road. The Black Rapids Glacier, which advanced four miles between 1963 and 1940, is visible from the Richardson Highway.

Glacier ice is blue because it has no air trapped in it, unlike snow or ice cubes from a freezer. Any air bubbles at the bottom of a snowpack are forced out by the weight of snow accumulating season after season at the top of a glacier. The six-sided crystals that result from such compression absorb most colors of the spectrum but reflect blue.

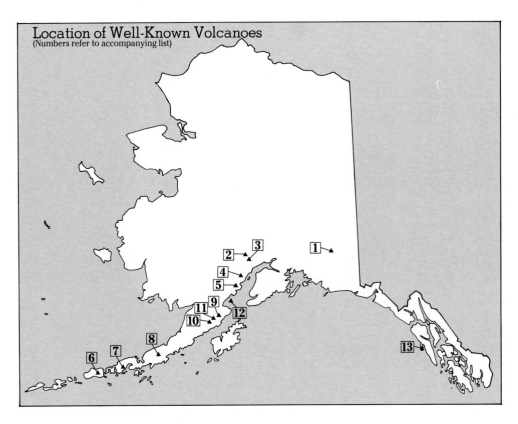

Location of Well-Known Volcanoes
(Numbers refer to accompanying list)

VOLCANOES

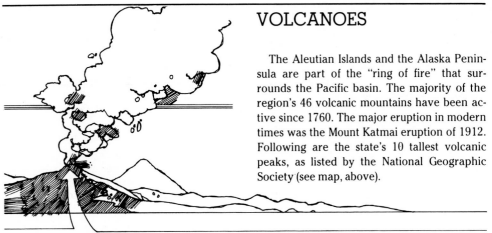

The Aleutian Islands and the Alaska Peninsula are part of the "ring of fire" that surrounds the Pacific basin. The majority of the region's 46 volcanic mountains have been active since 1760. The major eruption in modern times was the Mount Katmai eruption of 1912. Following are the state's 10 tallest volcanic peaks, as listed by the National Geographic Society (see map, above).

10 Highest Volcanic Peaks

	ELEVATION
Mount Wrangell (1)	14,163
Mount Torbert (2)	11,413
Mount Spurr (3)	11,069
Redoubt Volcano (4)	10,197
Iliamna Volcano (5)	10,016
Shishaldin Volcano (6)	9,372
Pavlof Volcano (7)	8,261
Mount Veniaminof (8)	8,225
Mount Griggs (9)	7,600
Mount Mageik (10)	7,250

Other Volcanic Peaks

	ELEVATION
Mount Katmai (11)	6,715
Augustine Volcano (12)	4,025
Mount Edgecumbe (13)	3,201

CLIMATE

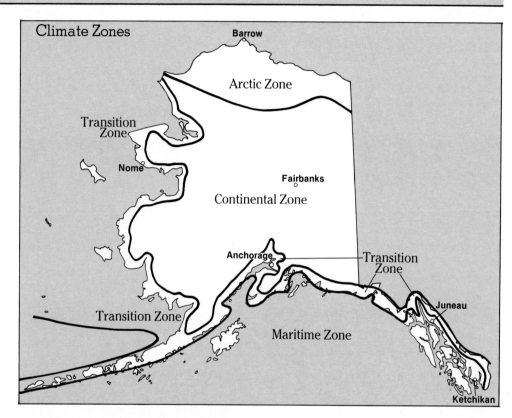

Climate Zones

Barrow

Arctic Zone

Transition Zone

Nome

Fairbanks

Continental Zone

Anchorage — Transition Zone

Transition Zone

Maritime Zone

Juneau

Ketchikan

Alaska's climate zones are maritime, transition, continental and arctic (see map, right.)

Maritime includes Southeastern, the Aleutian Chain and the immediate coastal area of the Gulf Coast. Temperatures are comparatively mild, and precipitation—mostly rain—is heavy, from 50 to 200 inches annually along the coast and up to 400 inches on the mountain slopes.

The Aleutians maintain a reputation as the windiest area in Alaska, with Amchitka being the windiest weather recording station in the state, followed by Cold Bay.

The roughest seas occur in the Gulf of Alaska. Waves up to 43 feet high have been reported south of Kodiak in midwinter, and waves of 50 feet in height south of Yakutat.

Transition, between maritime and continental, lies between the Coast Mountains and the Alaska Range and includes Anchorage and the Matanuska Valley, as well as the Bering Sea coast, which is too severe to be maritime but is milder than the Interior or Arctic. Summer temperatures are higher than the maritime climate, winter temperatures lower and precipitation less.

Continental covers the majority of the body of Alaska except the coastal fringes and Arctic Slope. It has extreme high and low temperatures and light precipitation.

Arctic, north of the Brooks Range, has cold winters, cool summers and desertlike precipitation. The arctic ice pack usually descends on shore in early October and retreats in mid-July to late August.

137

CLIMATE RECORDS

Highest temperature: 100°F, at Fort Yukon, June 27, 1915

Lowest temperature: -80°F, at Prospect Creek Camp, January 23, 1971

Most annual average precipitation: 332.29 inches, at MacLeod Harbour (Montague Island), 1976

Most precipitation in 24 hours: 14.84 inches, in Little Port Walter, December 6, 1964

Least precipitation in a year: 1.61 inches, at Barrow, 1935

Most snowfall in a season: 974.5 inches, at Thompson Pass, 1952-3

Most snowfall in 24 hours: 62 inches, at Thompson Pass, December 1955

Least snowfall in a season: 3 inches, at Barrow, 1935-6

Highest recorded snow depth in one season (also highest ever recorded in North America): 356 inches on Wolverine Glacier, Kenai Peninsula, after winter of 1976-7

Chill Factor

Wind chill can lower the effective temperature many degrees. While Alaska's regions of lowest temperatures also generally have little wind, activity such as riding a snowmobile or even walking can produce the same effect on exposed skin.

Chill Factor Table

TEMPERATURE (FAHRENHEIT)	EFFECTIVE TEMPERATURE WITH WIND SPEED OF . . .		
	10 mph	20 mph	30 mph
40	28	18	13
30	16	4	-2
20	4	-10	-18
10	-9	-25	-33
0	-21	-39	-48
-10	-33	-53	-63
-20	-46	-67	-79
-30	-58	-82	-94
-40	-70	-96	-109

Average Temperatures (Fahrenheit degrees) and Precipitation

	JUNEAU	JUNEAU WB AP	KETCHIKAN	CORDOVA FAA AP	SEWARD	VALDEZ	COLD BAY WB AP	ANCHORAGE WB AP	HOMER WSO	MATANUSKA AGR EXP STA	KING SALMON WB AP	BETHEL WB AP	NOME WB AP	FAIRBANKS WB AP	McGRATH WB AP
JANUARY															
Temperature	27.4°	23.5°	34.2°	23.0°	24.4°	17.8°	28.2°	11.8°	21.4°	11.9°	13.4°	5.1°	6.0°	-11.9°	-8.9°
Precipitation	6.89''	3.94''	15.06''	6.14''	4.60''	5.06''	2.42''	0.84''	1.70''	0.87''	0.94''	0.54''	0.90''	0.60''	0.85''
FEBRUARY															
Temperature	31.2°	28.0°	37.4°	26.7°	27.8°	22.4°	28.2°	17.8°	24.9°	19.1°	16.6°	8.2°	5.2°	-2.5°	-0.2°
Precipitation	6.16''	3.44''	12.74''	6.42''	5.43''	5.30''	2.59''	0.84''	1.54''	0.66''	0.99''	0.74''	0.84''	0.53''	0.90''
MARCH															
Temperature	34.7°	31.9°	38.8°	29.2°	30.8°	26.8°	29.0°	23.7°	27.6°	25.0°	20.4°	11.4°	7.4°	9.5°	8.9°
Precipitation	6.42''	3.57''	12.15''	5.89''	3.72''	4.33''	1.93''	0.56''	1.22''	0.50''	1.16''	0.79''	0.79''	0.48''	0.86''
APRIL															
Temperature	40.9°	38.9°	43.2°	36.0°	38.0°	35.6°	33.1°	35.3°	35.0°	36.4°	31.5°	24.5°	18.9°	28.9°	26.5°
Precipitation	5.99''	2.99''	12.88''	5.71''	3.48''	3.06''	1.54''	0.56''	1.09''	0.45''	0.90''	0.43''	0.73''	0.33''	0.66''
MAY															
Temperature	48.8°	46.8°	49.9°	43.7°	45.2°	43.8°	39.5°	46.2°	42.3°	47.0°	42.6°	40.1°	34.8°	47.3°	44.1°
Precipitation	5.61''	3.31''	8.62''	5.99''	3.48''	3.20''	2.19''	0.59''	0.91''	0.73''	1.13''	0.83''	0.70''	0.65''	0.80''
JUNE															
Temperature	55.2°	53.2°	55.1°	50.4°	52.0°	51.2°	45.4°	54.6°	48.7°	55.0°	50.7°	51.6°	45.5°	59.0°	55.7°
Precipitation	4.09''	2.93''	7.20''	4.67''	2.41''	2.70''	1.84''	1.07''	1.05''	1.64''	1.44''	1.24''	0.95''	1.42''	1.70''
JULY															
Temperature	57.4°	55.7°	58.3°	53.4°	56.0°	53.3°	50.1°	57.9°	52.3°	57.5°	54.5°	54.7°	50.1°	60.7°	58.2°
Precipitation	6.43''	4.69''	8.48''	7.08''	3.06''	4.31''	2.22''	2.07''	1.70''	2.43''	2.18''	1.98''	2.42''	1.90''	2.28''
AUGUST															
Temperature	56.5°	54.3°	58.6°	53.0°	55.8°	52.0°	51.3°	55.9°	52.4°	55.2°	53.8°	52.3°	49.2°	55.4°	53.5°
Precipitation	7.61''	5.00''	11.27''	8.94''	5.23''	5.80''	3.89''	2.32''	2.56''	2.74''	3.46''	3.97''	3.57''	2.19''	3.28''
SEPTEMBER															
Temperature	51.5°	49.2°	54.3°	48.0°	49.9°	46.5°	47.3°	48.1°	47.0°	47.7°	47.3°	45.0°	42.1°	44.4°	43.8°
Precipitation	11.08''	6.90''	15.28''	13.53''	9.43''	7.74''	3.95''	2.37''	2.85''	2.28''	3.07''	2.42''	2.40''	1.05''	2.14''
OCTOBER															
Temperature	43.9°	41.8°	47.2°	39.6°	39.8°	37.5°	39.6°	34.8°	37.4°	34.5°	33.6°	30.2°	28.5°	25.2°	25.3°
Precipitation	13.36''	7.85''	24.77''	12.34''	9.33''	6.75''	4.31''	1.43''	3.38''	1.35''	2.00''	1.32''	1.42''	0.73''	1.22''
NOVEMBER															
Temperature	35.3°	32.5°	40.4°	30.6°	30.9°	26.1°	34.3°	21.1°	28.2°	20.7°	22.1°	17.2°	15.6°	2.8°	5.0°
Precipitation	10.00''	5.53''	17.63''	8.37''	6.73''	5.67''	3.90''	1.02''	2.76''	0.89''	1.43''	0.95''	0.98''	0.66''	1.03''
DECEMBER															
Temperature	30.4°	27.3°	36.4°	24.6°	24.8°	19.5°	29.0°	13.0°	21.4°	12.5°	11.7°	4.4°	4.4°	-10.4°	-9.2°
Precipitation	8.39''	4.52''	16.18''	7.45''	6.45''	5.39''	2.45''	1.07''	2.29''	0.89''	1.05''	0.62''	0.74''	0.65''	1.02''
ANNUAL															
Temperature	42.8°	40.3°	46.2°	38.2°	39.6°	36.0°	37.9°	35.0°	36.5°	35.2°	33.2°	28.7°	25.6°	25.1°	25.2°
Precipitation	91.98''	54.67''	162.27''	92.53''	63.35''	59.31''	33.23''	14.74''	23.06''	15.43''	19.75''	15.84''	16.44''	11.22''	16.74''

Key: AGR EXP STA—Agriculture Experimental Station AP—Airport FAA—Federal Aviation Agency WB—Weather Bureau WSO—Weather Service Office

TOWNS AND VILLAGES

Alaska's 400,000-plus residents are distributed among more than 330 towns and villages from Ketchikan to Barrow—with more than half in the Anchorage trading area. Three-fourths of the state's residents live in the 14 communities with a population over 2,000—the remainder are largely in villages with fewer than 500 people. The vast majority of Alaska's towns and villages are along seacoasts or rivers. Relatively few are connected to the state's modest highway system.

CENSUS DIVISIONS

These July 1, 1978, population estimates (by census divisions, not municipal boundaries) were made by the Research and Analysis Section of the Alaska Department of Labor. Note: These estimates were developed using a new method. For this reason, 1978 levels are not comparable to prior year estimates and should not be used for trends analysis.

Aleutian Islands	8,000
Anchorage	185,500
Angoon	600
Barrow	8,300
Bethel	10,000
Bristol Bay	3,900
Bristol Bay Borough	1,400
Cordova-McCarthy	2,400
Fairbanks	55,500
Haines	1,500
Juneau	19,500
Kenai-Cook Inlet	22,300
Ketchikan	12,600
Kobuk	5,300
Kodiak	9,600
Kuskokwim	2,700
Matanuska-Susitna	15,400
Nome	7,200
Outer Ketchikan	2,000
Prince of Wales	2,600
Seward	3,100
Sitka	7,200
Skagway-Yakutat	2,800
Southeast Fairbanks	5,300
Upper Yukon	1,200
Valdez-Chitina-Whittier	5,000
Wade Hampton	4,400
Wrangell-Petersburg	5,600
Yukon-Koyukuk	5,500
Total State:	416,400

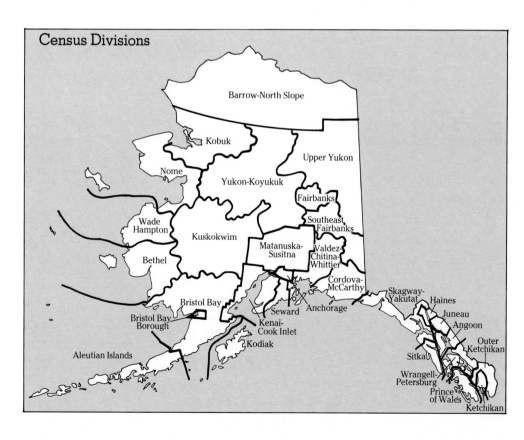

Census Divisions

Age and Gender of Alaskans
Median age about 22
Men: 54.35% of population
Women: 45.64% of population

Alaskans by Age

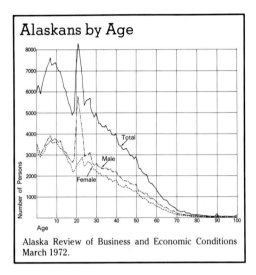

Alaska Review of Business and Economic Conditions March 1972.

Of people age 14 or over, the Bureau of the Census showed:
Men: 113,657; 33.8% single; 60.7% married; 5.5% widowed or divorced
Women: 89,907; 20.5% single; 71.5% married; 8.0% widowed or divorced

Births and Deaths
According to the Alaska Department of Health and Social Services, in 1978 there were 8,378 births, 1,607 deaths, 5,143 marriages, 3,581 divorces, 727 adoptions and 1,074 abortions.

POPULATIONS AND ZIP CODES

Alaska's population at the time of the 1970 census was 302,361. A July 1978 estimate by the Alaska Department of Labor placed the state's population at 416,400. The following list of communities shows those places recorded in the 1970 census as having more than 25 people, plus additional zip-coded localities. Because of seasonal variations in populations and census district variances, census figures are not exact. Figures are sometimes not available on the percentage of the population that is Native. In such circumstances the list shows NA (not available).

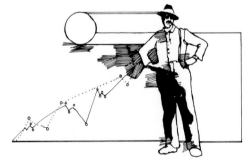

COMMUNITY	1970 POPULATION		
	TOTAL	NATIVE	ZIP CODE
Adak	2,249	54	99695
Akhiok	115	114	99615
Akiachak	312	300	99551
Akiak	171	169	99552
Akolmiut	526	512	99695
Akutan	101	87	99553
Alakanuk	265	246	99554
Aleknagik	128	95	99555
Alexander Creek	NA	NA	99695
Alitak	NA	NA	99697
Allakaket	174	168	99720
Ambler	169	159	99786
Amchitka	NA	NA	99501
Anaktuvuk Pass	99	97	99721
Anchor Point	102	NA	99556
Anchorage area	124,542	4,795	995--
	185,500**	-	-
Anderson	362	7	99790
Angoon	400	377	99820
Aniak	205	170	99557
Annette	195	19	99920
Anvik	83	75	99558
Arctic Village	85	82	99722
Atka	88	86	99502
Atmautluak	107*	107*	99559
Auke Bay	490	NA	99821
Aurora-Johnston	1,464	NA	99701
Baranof	NA	NA	99833
Barrow	2,104	1,906	99723
Beaver	101	86	99724
Belkofski	59	51	99695
Bethel	2,416	1,871	99559
Big Lake	448	NA	99695
Big Mountain	NA	NA	99695
Birch Creek	40	36	99790
Birchwood	1,219	107	99501

*Estimate **1978 Estimate

COMMUNITY	1970 POPULATION TOTAL	NATIVE	ZIP CODE
Boundary	NA	NA	99790
Broadmoor	402	NA	99701
Buckland	104	103	99727
Butte	448	NA	99695
Campbell	40	6	99950
Candle	NA	NA	99728
Cantwell	62	43	99729
Cape Lisburne	83	NA	99790
Cape Pole	123	15	99950
Cape Sarachef	NA	NA	99695
Cape Yakataga	NA	NA	99560
Central	26	3	99730
Chalkyitsik	130	123	99788
Chatanika	NA	NA	99731
Chuathbaluk (Little Russian Mission)	94	90	99557
Chefornak	146	141	99561
Chevak	387	376	99563
Chicken	32	NA	99732
Chignik	83	63	99564
Chignik Lagoon	45*	NA	99565
Chignik Lake	117	115	99502
Chistochina	33	17	99586
Chitina	38	6	99566
Chugiak	489	5	99567
Circle	54	32	99733
Clam Gulch	47	NA	99568
Clarks Point	95	75	99569
Clear	362	36	99704
Clover Pass	261	NA	99901
Cohoe	NA	NA	99570
Cold Bay	256	25	99571
College	3,434	NA	99701
Cooper Landing	31	1	99572
Copper Center	206	93	99573
Cordova	1,164	190	99574

*Estimate

COMMUNITY	1970 POPULATION TOTAL	NATIVE	ZIP CODE
Craig	272	153	99921
Crooked Creek	59	55	99575
Deadhorse	163	15	99790
Deering	85	83	99736
Delta Junction	703	10	99737
Dillingham	914	569	99576
Dot Lake	42	29	99737
Douglas	1,243	NA	99824
Dutch Harbor	50*	NA	99695
Eagle	103	58	99738
Eagle River	2,437	NA	99577
Edna Bay	112	3	99950
Eek	186	167	99578
Egegik	148	71	99579
Eielson Air Force Base	6,149	NA	99702
Eklutna	25	23	99790
Ekuk	51	50	99595
Ekwok	103	94	99580
Elephant Point	104	NA	99790
Elfin Cove	49	2	99825
Elim	174	168	99739
Elmendorf Air Force Base	6,018	39	99506
Emanguk	439	421	99581
English Bay	58	53	99603
Ester	264	NA	99725
Evansville	57	14	99726
Excursion Inlet	NA	NA	99850
Fairbanks area	45,864† 55,500**	1,876† -	997-- -
False Pass	62	58	99583
Farmers Loop	110	NA	99701
Fire Lake	475	NA	99695
Flat	NA	NA	99584
Fort Greely	1,820	NA	99790
Fort Richardson	8,960	173	99505
Fort Wainwright	9,097	NA	99703

*Estimate **1978 estimate
†Inside City Limits: 14,771 total, 925 Native.

COMMUNITY	1970 POPULATION TOTAL	NATIVE	ZIP CODE
Fort Yukon	448	376	99740
Fritz Cove	296	NA	99801
Fritz Creek	27	NA	99697
Gakona	88	23	99586
Galena	302	265	99741
Gambell	372	356	99742
Girdwood	144	NA	99587
Glennallen	363	37	99588
Golovin	117	111	99762
Goodnews	218	210	99589
Graehl	348	NA	99701
Granite Mountain	NA	NA	99790
Grayling	139	136	99590
Gulkana	53	52	99695
Gustavus	64	4	99826
Haines	463	110	99827
Halibut Cove	44	NA	99603
Hawk Inlet	NA	NA	99850
Healy	79	10	99743
Herring Cove	114	NA	99901
Hogatza	NA	NA	99744
Holy Cross	199	192	99602
Homer	1,083	52	99603
Hoonah	748	539	99829
Hooper Bay	490	477	99604
Hope	51	0	99605
Houston	69	2	99697
Hughes	85	73	99745
Huslia	159	151	99746
Hydaburg	214	189	99922
Hyder	79	0	99923
Idaho Inlet	NA	NA	99850
Igiugig	36	34	99613
Iliamna	58	23	99606
Ivanof Bay	48	46	99695

COMMUNITY	1970 POPULATION TOTAL	NATIVE	ZIP CODE
Juneau	13,556	1,745	998--
	19,500**	-	-
Kachemak	76	12	99790
Kaguyak	59	33	99880
Kake	448	406	99830
Kakhonak	88	67	99606
Kaktovik	123	108	99747
Kalskag	122	106	99607
Kaltag	206	193	99748
Karluk	98	95	99608
Kasaan	30	8	99901
Kashega	26	NA	99697
Kasilof	71	0	99610
Kenai	3,533	175	99611
Ketchikan	6,994	1,078	99901
Kiana	278	268	99749
King Cove	283	244	99612
King Salmon	202	12	99613
Kipnuk	325	320	99614
Kitoi Bay	NA	NA	99697
Kivalina	188	183	99750
Klawock	213	195	99925
Klukwan	103	92	99827
Kobuk	60*	57*	99751
Kodiak	3,798	642	99615
Kodiak Naval Station	3,052	NA	98791
Koggiung	70	NA	99695
Koliganek	142	134	99576
Kongiganak	190	183	99559
Kotik	228	224	99620
Kotzebue	1,696	1,325	99752
Koyuk	122	121	99753
Koyukuk	124	121	99754
Kwethluk	408	390	99621
Kwigillingok	148	145	99622
Lake Minchumina	NA	NA	99623

COMMUNITY	1970 POPULATION TOTAL	NATIVE	ZIP CODE
Larsen Bay	109	91	99624
Lemeta	1,318	NA	99701
Lemon Creek	1,042	NA	99801
Lena Cove	300	NA	99801
Levelock	74	60	99625
Lime Village	25	25	99695
Little Diomede Village	84	82	99762
Livengood	NA	NA	99790
Lower Kalsag	183	177	99626
Lower Mendenhall Valley	1,109	NA	99801
Manley Hot Springs	34	11	99756
Manokotak	214	205	99628
Marshall	175	169	99585
McGrath	279	110	99627
McKinley Park	26	NA	99755
Meakerville	349	NA	99574
Medfra	NA	NA	99629
Mekoryuk	249	234	99630
Mendenhall Flats	164	NA	99801
Mentasta Lake	68	64	99780
Metlakatla	1,050	847	99926
Meyers Chuck	37	2	99903
Minto	168	159	99758
Montana	33	4	99695
Moose Pass	53	0	99631
Moser Bay	NA	NA	99697
Mountain Point	459	NA	99950
Mountain View	NA	NA	99504
Mountain Village	419	394	99632
Mount Edgecumbe	835	483	99835

COMMUNITY	1970 POPULATION TOTAL	NATIVE	ZIP CODE
Mud Bay	103	NA	99901
Naknek	178	38	99633
Napakiak	270	265	99634
Napaskiak	259	255	99559
Nelson Lagoon	43	39	99697
Nenana	362	142	99760
New Stuyahok	216	208	99636
Newhalen	88	83	99695
Newtok	114	111	99559
Nightmute	127	122	99690
Nikishka	NA	NA	99661
Nikolai	112	101	99691
Nikolski	57	52	99638
Ninilchik	134	18	99639
Noatak	293	286	99761
Nome	2,488	1,534	99762
Nondalton	184	182	99640
Noorvik	462	443	99763
North Douglas	538	NA	99801
North Pole	265	26	99705
Northeast Cape	NA	NA	99790
Northway	120	10	99764
Nulato	308	298	99765
Old Harbor	290	269	99643
Oscarville	41	38	99695
Ouzinkie	160	143	99644
Palmer	1,140	35	99645
Pauloff Harbor	39	38	99646
Paxson	NA	NA	99737
Pedro Bay	65	51	99647
Pelican	133	27	99832
Peninsula Point	175	NA	99901
Pennock Island	78	NA	99950
Perryville	94	90	99648
Peters Creek	340	NA	99790

*Estimate **Area, 1978 estimate.

COMMUNITY	1970 POPULATION TOTAL	NATIVE	ZIP CODE
Petersburg	2,042	295	99833
Pilot Point	68	58	99649
Pilot Station	290	287	99650
Pitkas Point	70	67	99658
Platinum	55	48	99651
Point Baker	NA	NA	99927
Point Hope	386	369	99766
Point Lay	NA	NA	99790
Port Alexander	36	3	99833
Port Alsworth	NA	NA	99653
Port Ashton	NA	NA	99654
Port Chilkoot	220	52	99827
Port Graham	107	96	99695
Port Heiden	66	58	99549
Port Higgins	189	NA	99901
Port Lions	227	184	99550
Port Moller	NA	NA	99695
Port Protection	NA	NA	99950
Port William	NA	NA	99697
Portage Creek	75	NA	99576
Prudhoe Bay	49	4	99716
Quinhagak	340	332	99655
Rampart	36	21	99767
Red Devil	81	22	99656
Ruby	145	134	99768
Russian Mission	146	138	99657
Saint George Island	163	154	99660
Saint Marys	384	350	99658
Saint Michael	207	192	99659
Saint Paul Island	450	422	99660
Salmon Creek	302	NA	99801
Sand Lake	4,168	NA	99502
Sand Point	360	245	99661
Savoonga	364	354	99769
Saxman	135	99	99950

COMMUNITY	1970 POPULATION TOTAL	NATIVE	ZIP CODE
Scammon Bay	166	166	99662
Scow Bay	238	NA	99850
Selawik	429	418	99770
Seldovia	437	129	99663
Seward	1,587	216	99664
Shageluk	167	158	99665
Shaktoolik	151	144	99771
Sheldon Point	125	121	99666
Shemya Island	1,131	NA	99695
Shishmaref	267	249	99772
Shungnak	165	160	99773
Sitka	4,205	1,246	99835
Skagway	675	41	99840
Skwentna	NA	NA	99667
Sleetmute	109	95	99668
Soldotna	1,202	16	99669
South Naknek	154	85	99670
Squaw Harbor	65	44	99661
Stebbins	231	223	99671
Sterling	130	NA	99672
Stevens Village	74	72	99774
Stony River	74	61	99557
Summit	34	2	99775
Suntrana	67	11	99790
Sutton	76	3	99674
Takotna	36*	19	99675
Talkeetna	182	12	99676
Tanacross	84	77	99776
Tanana	411	350	99777
Tanunak	274	270	99681
Tatitlek	111	107	99677
Teller	220	192	99778
Teller Mission	123	118	99785
Tenakee Springs	86	10	99841
Tetlin	114	108	99779

*Estimate.

COMMUNITY	1970 POPULATION TOTAL	NATIVE	ZIP CODE
Thorne Bay	443	7	99950
Togiak	383	377	99678
Tok	214	26	99780
Toksook Bay	257	251	99637
Tuluksak	195	193	99679
Tuntutuliak	158	154	99680
Twin Hills	67	66	99695
Tyonek	235	221	99682
Ugashik	NA	NA	99683
Unalakleet	434	403	99684
Unalaska	178	110	99685
Upper Mendenhall Valley	1,815	NA	99801
Usibelli	102	14	99787
Valdez	1,005	133	99686
Venetie	112	108	99781
Wainwright	315	307	99782
Wales	131	121	99783
Ward Cove	105	NA	99928
Wasilla	300	3	99687
West Petersburg (Kupreanof)	36	NA	99850
White Mountain	87	84	99784
Whittier	130	5	99501
Wildwood	750	NA	99611
Willow	38	NA	99688
Wiseman	NA	NA	99726
Woody Island	41	NA	99697
Wrangell	2,029	421	99929
Yakutat	190	157	99689
Yes Bay	NA	NA	99950

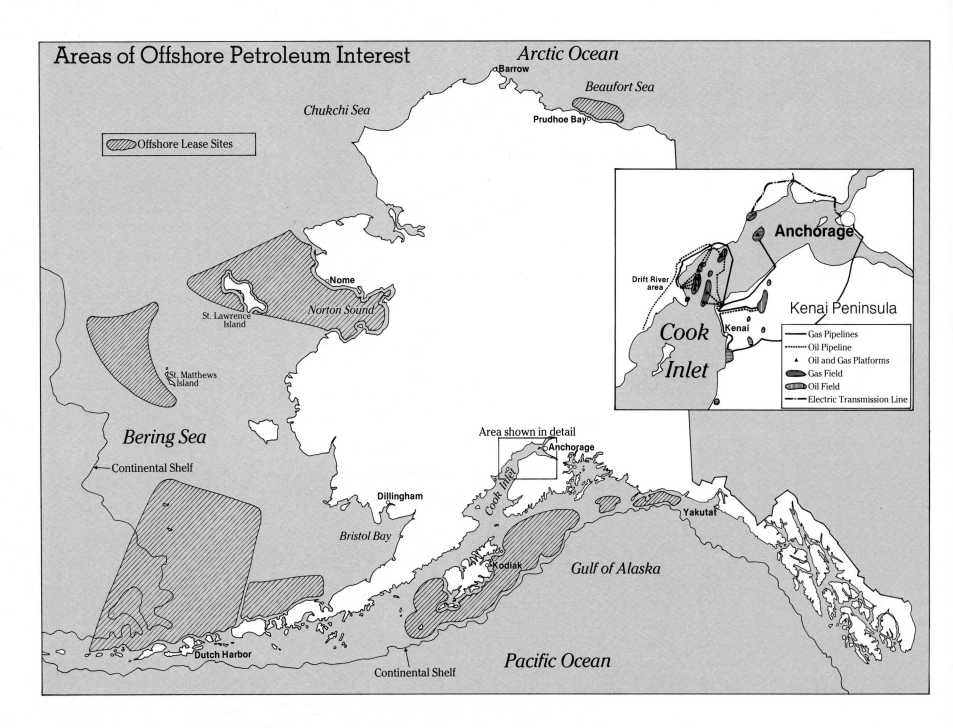

Areas of Offshore Petroleum Interest

Arctic Ocean

Barrow

Beaufort Sea

Chukchi Sea

Prudhoe Bay

Offshore Lease Sites

Nome

Norton Sound

St. Lawrence Island

St. Matthews Island

Bering Sea

← Continental Shelf

Dillingham

Bristol Bay

Kodiak

Gulf of Alaska

Yakutat

Anchorage

Area shown in detail

Cook Inlet

Continental Shelf

Dutch Harbor

Pacific Ocean

Anchorage

Drift River area

Cook Inlet

Kenai Peninsula

Kenai

—— Gas Pipelines

······ Oil Pipeline

▲ Oil and Gas Platforms

⬭ Gas Field

▥ Oil Field

—·— Electric Transmission Line

INDUSTRIES

OIL AND GAS

Alaska's dominant industry—at least in terms of dollars contributed to the state treasury—is oil and gas, which is responsible for a large percentage of the state's annual budget. The vast majority of this money was coming from royalties earned from North Slope oil production.

Although considered a modern addition to the industrial scene in Alaska, oil and gas exploration and production have been around for a long time.

Alaska's first exploratory oil well was drilled in 1900 on the Iniskin Peninsula, Cook Inlet, by Alaska Petroleum Company. According to the Alaska Oil & Gas Association, oil was encountered in this first hole at about 700 feet, but a water zone beneath the oil strata cut off the oil flow. Total depth of the well was approximately 1,000 feet.

The first commercial oil discovery was made in 1902 near Katalla, near the mouth of the Bering River east of Cordova. This field produced until 1933.

As early as 1921 oil companies surveyed land north of the Brooks Range for possible drilling sites. In 1923 the federal government created Naval Petroleum Reserve Number Four (now known as Naval Petroleum Reserve—Alaska), a 37,000-square-mile area of Alaska's North Slope. Wartime needs speeded up exploration. In 1944 the navy began drilling operations on the North Slope and continued until 1953, but made no significant oil discoveries.

Atlantic Richfield discovered oil in 1957 on the Kenai Peninsula, at a depth of approximately 3 miles, near the headwaters of the Swanson River, about 20 miles northeast of Kenai. Later Union Oil found a large gas field at Kalifonsky Beach, and Shell found the first oil offshore at a location known as Middle Ground Shoals in Cook Inlet.

At present there are 14 production platforms in Cook Inlet, one of which produces only gas. Built to contend with extreme tides, siltation and ice floes, the Cook Inlet platforms are in one of three successful areas of offshore oil production in the United States. Hundreds of miles of pipeline, with diameters of up to 20 inches, link the offshore platforms with onshore facilities at Kenai, Drift River and Anchorage. Gas reserves in the Kenai gas field are estimated to be the third largest in the United States. The deepest producing oil well in the state is at Soldotna Creek on the Kenai Peninsula; depth is 17,689 feet. A fertilizer plant, largest of its kind on the West Coast, is located at Kenai. It uses natural gas as a feed stock to manufacture 3,100 tons per day of ammonia and 2,500 tons per day of urea. The plant daily processes 160 million cubic feet of gas. Two refineries are located at Kenai; a third is at North Pole. Gasoline, diesel fuel, heavy fuel oil, JP-4, Jet A-50 and asphalt—are produced for use within and outside Alaska.

The Prudhoe Bay oil field, largest in North America, was discovered in 1968 by Atlantic-Richfield. Recoverable reserves, according to Sohio BP-Alaska, are estimated to be 9.4 billion barrels of oil and 26.5 trillion cubic feet of hydrocarbon gas. At the end of 1978, the first full year of production, 450 million barrels had been produced from the field. The field contains about one-quarter of the known petroleum reserves in the United States. By the end of 1978, 159 producing and 18 service wells had been completed. Two operators, Sohio BP-Alaska, which manages the western portion of the field, and ARCO, which manages the eastern portion of the field, act on behalf of 16 participant companies.

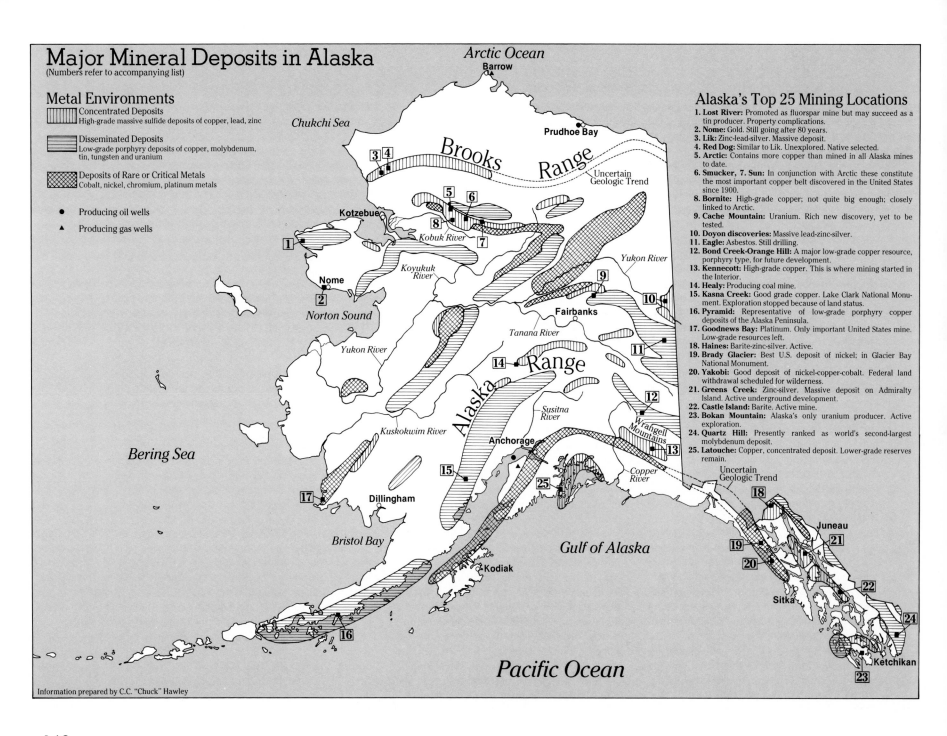

Major Mineral Deposits in Alaska
(Numbers refer to accompanying list)

Metal Environments

Concentrated Deposits
High-grade massive sulfide deposits of copper, lead, zinc

Disseminated Deposits
Low-grade porphyry deposits of copper, molybdenum, tin, tungsten and uranium

Deposits of Rare or Critical Metals
Cobalt, nickel, chromium, platinum metals

● Producing oil wells

▲ Producing gas wells

Arctic Ocean

Barrow

Chukchi Sea

Prudhoe Bay

Brooks Range

Uncertain Geologic Trend

Kotzebue

Kobuk River

Koyukuk River

Yukon River

Nome

Norton Sound

Yukon River

Fairbanks

Tanana River

Range

Alaska

Susitna River

Kuskokwim River

Anchorage

Wrangell Mountains

Copper River

Uncertain Geologic Trend

Bering Sea

Dillingham

Bristol Bay

Gulf of Alaska

Juneau

Sitka

Kodiak

Ketchikan

Pacific Ocean

Alaska's Top 25 Mining Locations

1. **Lost River:** Promoted as fluorspar mine but may succeed as a tin producer. Property complications.
2. **Nome:** Gold. Still going after 80 years.
3. **Lik:** Zinc-lead-silver. Massive deposit.
4. **Red Dog:** Similar to Lik. Unexplored. Native selected.
5. **Arctic:** Contains more copper than mined in all Alaska mines to date.
6. **Smucker, 7. Sun:** In conjunction with Arctic these constitute the most important copper belt discovered in the United States since 1900.
8. **Bornite:** High-grade copper; not quite big enough; closely linked to Arctic.
9. **Cache Mountain:** Uranium. Rich new discovery, yet to be tested.
10. **Doyon discoveries:** Massive lead-zinc-silver.
11. **Eagle:** Asbestos. Still drilling.
12. **Bond Creek-Orange Hill:** A major low-grade copper resource, porphyry type, for future development.
13. **Kennecott:** High-grade copper. This is where mining started in the Interior.
14. **Healy:** Producing coal mine.
15. **Kasna Creek:** Good grade copper. Lake Clark National Monument. Exploration stopped because of land status.
16. **Pyramid:** Representative of low-grade porphyry copper deposits of the Alaska Peninsula.
17. **Goodnews Bay:** Platinum. Only important United States mine. Low-grade resources left.
18. **Haines:** Barite-zinc-silver. Active.
19. **Brady Glacier:** Best U.S. deposit of nickel; in Glacier Bay National Monument.
20. **Yakobi:** Good deposit of nickel-copper-cobalt. Federal land withdrawal scheduled for wilderness.
21. **Greens Creek:** Zinc-silver. Massive deposit on Admiralty Island. Active underground development.
22. **Castle Island:** Barite. Active mine.
23. **Bokan Mountain:** Alaska's only uranium producer. Active exploration.
24. **Quartz Hill:** Presently ranked as world's second-largest molybdenum deposit.
25. **Latouche:** Copper, concentrated deposit. Lower-grade reserves remain.

Information prepared by C.C. "Chuck" Hawley

146

HARD-ROCK MINING

Total value of hard mineral production in Alaska amounted to almost $160 million in 1977, compared with $67.7 million in 1975, according to figures compiled by the U.S. Department of the Interior, Bureau of Mines and the Division of Economic Enterprise, Department of Commerce and Economic Development. Sand and gravel worth $205 million were extracted in 1976, as compared to almost $5.3 million worth of sand and gravel extracted in 1959. The value dropped to $134 million in 1977 due to slowing of construction. Almost $2.9 million of gold was mined in 1977, as compared to approximately $6.3 million in 1959. The extraction of barite, bituminous coal, gemstones, lead, silver, stone, copper, mercury, natural gas liquids, platinum-group metals and tin totaled approximately $23 million in 1977 and was slightly more than $8.6 million in 1959.

FURS AND TRAPPING

Most of the state's trapping is done in the Yukon-Kuskokwim valleys and in the Arctic. It is seasonal work, so most trappers, represented by an equal number of Natives and whites, work summers at fishing or other employment. In 1979, the three best money furs were wolf (up to $500), lynx (to $450) and wolverine ($400). Mink, muskrat, and fox furs are more plentiful. Trapping is subject to Alaska Department of Fish & Game regulations.

TIMBER

According to the Alaska Loggers Association, Alaska has 2 distinct forest ecosystems: the coastal rain forest and the interior forest. The vast interior forest covers 106 million acres, extending from the south slope of the Brooks Range to the Kenai Peninsula, and from Canada to Norton Sound. Over 22 million acres of white spruce, paper birch, quaking aspen and balsam poplar stands are considered commercial forest land, comparing favorably in size and growth productivity with the forests of the lake states (Minnesota, Michigan and Wisconsin). The interior forest's present remoteness from markets and land management policies have limited timber use to approximately 50 small local sawmills with limited export of cants and chips.

The coastal rain forests extend from Cook Inlet to the Alaska-Canada border south of Ketchikan and provide the bulk of commercial timber in Alaska today. Of the 13,247,000 acres of forested land, 5,749,000 acres contain commercial stands. Western hemlock, 70% of the total, and Sitka spruce, 25% of the total, provide the bulk of the timber harvest for domestic and export lumber and pulp markets. Western red cedar and Alaska (yellow) cedar make up the balance, with pine and other species also present. Logging, pulp mills and sawmills employed 3,426 workers in 1977, with a product value of approximately $225 million. Since 1903, approximately 300,000 acres of coastal forest land have been harvested, less than 5% of the potential commercial stands.

TOURISM

The business of tourism, growing at a steady 10-15% per year through the 1970's, has become the state's second leading industry—in terms of dollars generated—behind the oil and gas industry. In 1979, it was estimated that tourists spent about $330 million in their travels to and throughout Alaska.

State officials estimated that 600,000 visitors came to the state during 1979, approximately 465,000 on vacation and 135,000 on business-related trips.

The trend in recent years has been toward increased air travel, but travel by state ferry, cruise ship and highway—either in private vehicles or with bus lines—has also increased steadily.

(For specific information on air, sea and highway travel to and within Alaska, see "Transportation," page 152.)

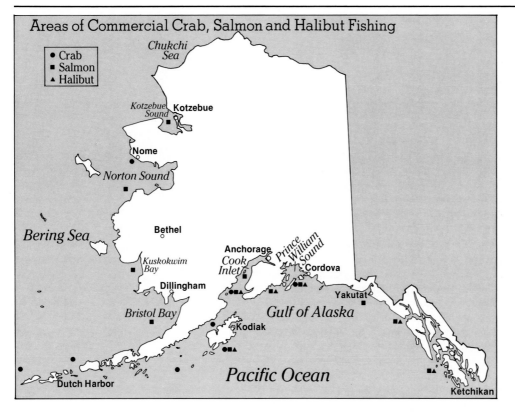

Areas of Commercial Crab, Salmon and Halibut Fishing

- ● Crab
- ■ Salmon
- ▲ Halibut

COMMERCIAL FISHING

Alaska's commercial fish production is greater than that of any other state in the country in terms of value and second in terms of volume. (Louisiana is first in volume.)

In 1978, according to statistics compiled by the National Marine Fisheries Service, commercial fish landings in Alaska totaled 745.6 million pounds and were valued at $438.6 million. California was second ($228.2 million), followed by Louisiana ($190.2 million), Massachusetts ($152.3 million) and Texas ($148.9 million).

Dutch Harbor was the leading U.S. port in terms of value, claiming $99.7 million in commercial fish landings, including 91 million pounds of king crab. Kodiak was second ($92.6 million), followed by San Pedro, California ($92.1 million), San Diego, California ($69.8 million), and New Bedford, Massachusetts ($54.6 million). Other Alaska ports in the top 50 nationwide in terms of value were Ketchikan, ranked 12th ($26.4 million); Akutan, 18th ($21.2 million) and Petersburg, 23rd ($17.5 million).

Alaska pollack and other Alaska trawl fish landings by U.S. fishermen were 5.5 million pounds valued at $729,000, up 98% in quantity and 115% in value from 1977. The total foreign catch of trawl fish in Alaska waters was 3.4 billion pounds, up 15%. About 90% of the catch came from the Bering Sea; the rest was caught in the Gulf of Alaska.

King crab landings of 130.2 million pounds, valued at $168.1 million to the fishermen, were the second highest in history, surpassed only by the 1965 landings of 159.2 million pounds. Landings from the Bering Sea were

Commercial Salmon Landings in Alaska (Numbers are in thousands)

	KING	RED	SILVER	PINK	CHUM	TOTAL
SOUTHEASTERN						
1978 Landings*	389	692	1,573	19,988	597	23,239
1962-76 Average	301	790	1,089	11,100	1,843	15,123
CENTRAL (Prince William Sound to south side of Alaska Peninsula)						
1978 Landings*	55	6,483	658	26,622	2,605	36,423
1962-76 Average	33	3,593	508	13,801	2,505	20,440
WESTERN (North Side Alaska Peninsula to Kotzebue)						
1978 Landings*	350	10,612	383	6,058	3,166	20,569
1962-76 Average	234	7,326	162	979	1,290	9,991

*Figures are preliminary

113.3 million pounds. A record 131.3 million pounds of snow (tanner) crabs, valued at $52.6 million, were taken from the Bering Sea and the Gulf of Alaska; Japanese fishermen harvested an additional 33 million pounds.

Alaska landings of shrimp were 74.5 million pounds, a decrease of 42.5 million pounds compared with 1977.

In 1978, Alaska commercial fishermen landed 349.3 million pounds of salmon, up 27% over 1977, and the largest since 1940. Pink salmon landings (194 million pounds) were the second largest on record, only 837,000 pounds less than 1918, the record year.

The chart on page 148 lists numbers of salmon (in thousands) caught per region. Note: 1978 catch figures are preliminary.

GOVERNMENT

One of Alaska's most reliable "growth industries" is government, which has managed to expand rapidly even as hard times hit some other industries. Expansion of government agencies and services has been especially rapid during the 1970's and today government employment—federal, state, borough, local and military—directly or indirectly supports more than 40% of the state's residents.

Here is a brief rundown on government operations in Alaska:

Alaska is represented in the U.S. Congress by two senators, one representative.

Governor and lieutenant governor are elected by popular vote for four-year terms on the same ticket. Governor is termed "strong" because of extensive powers given under the constitution. He administers 14 major departments: Administration, Commerce & Economic Development, Community and Regional Affairs, Education, Environmental Conservation, Fish & Game, Health and Social Services, Labor, Law, Military Affairs, Natural Resources, Public Safety, Revenue, Transportation and Public Facilities.

Legislature is bicameral, with 20 senators elected for four-year terms, 40 representatives for two-year terms. Judiciary consists of state supreme court, superior court, district courts, and magistrates.

Local government is by a system of organized boroughs, much like counties in other states. Several areas of the state are not included in any borough because of sparse population. Boroughs generally provide a more limited number of services than cities. There are three classes. First- and second-class boroughs have two mandatory powers: educa-

tion and land use planning. The major difference between the two classes is how they may acquire other powers. Both classes have separately elected borough assemblies and school boards. A third-class borough has one mandatory power: operation of public schools. All boroughs may assess, levy, and collect real and personal property taxes. (Borough addresses are listed on page 150.)

Incorporated cities are small units of local government, serving one community. There are two classes. First-class cities, generally urban areas, have six-member councils and a separately elected mayor. Taxing authority is somewhat broader than second-class cities, and responsibilities are broader. A first-class city that has adopted a home rule charter is called a home rule city; adoption allows the city to revise its ordinances, such that the powers which it assumes are those not prohibited by law or charter. Second-class cities, generally places with fewer than 400 people, are governed by a seven-member council, one of whom serves as mayor. Taxing authority is limited. A borough and all cities located within it may unite in a single unit of government called a united municipality.

There is also one community organized under federal law. Originally an Indian reservation, Metlakatla was organized so municipal services could effectively be provided.

By 1979 there was a total of 151 incorporated municipalities: 3 unified home rule municipalities, 1 home rule borough, 6 second-class boroughs, 1 third-class borough, 11 home rule cities, 21 first-class cities, 107 second-class cities and one community, Metlakatla, organized under federal law.

Borough Addresses and Contact

The City and Borough of Juneau
Contact: City-Borough Manager
155 South Seward Street
Juneau 99801

Fairbanks North Star Borough
Contact: Clerk
512 Second Avenue
P.O. Box 1267
Fairbanks 99701

Kodiak Island Borough
*Contact: Borough Mayor or
Borough Clerk*
P.O. Box 1246
Kodiak 99615

Haines Borough
Contact: Borough Secretary
Box H
Haines 99827

Municipality of Anchorage
*Contact: Mayor's Office or
Manager's Office*
524 West Fourth Avenue
Pouch 6-650
Anchorage 99502

Kenai Peninsula Borough
Contact: Borough Clerk
P.O. Box 850
Soldotna 99669

Bristol Bay Borough
Contact: Borough Clerk
P.O. Box 189
Naknek 99633

Matanuska-Susitna Borough
Contact: Borough Manager
Box B
Palmer 99645

North Slope Borough
Contact: Borough Mayor
P.O. Box 69
Barrow 99723

City and Borough of Sitka
Contact: Administrator
P.O. Box 79
Sitka 99835

Ketchikan Gateway Borough
Contact: Borough Manager
344 Front Street
Ketchikan 99901

AGRICULTURE

As of the 1974 U.S. census of agriculture, Alaska had 1,600,000 acres of farmland, about 70,000 acres of which were tillable. The 300 farms averaged 4,831.9 acres.

In 1977, 19,268 acres were planted. An estimated 210 farms produced crops valued at $9.8 million. According to the state Division of Agriculture, principal crops produced were:

Milk	$2,957,000
Hay	2,781,000
Potatoes	1,265,000
Eggs	620,000
Barley	479,000
Beef	477,000
Reindeer meat, by-products	471,000
Silage	433,000
Lettuce	263,000
Pork	161,000

The Tanana Valley produces most of the remaining 25% of total crop sales. Its growing season is shorter, with 90 frost-free days, and low precipitation levels make irrigation necessary for some crops. However, this region has the greatest agricultural potential, with warmer temperatures during the growing season and the presence of large tracts of reasonably flat land with brush rather than forest growth. Also, an increasing amount of Matanuska Valley acreage is being taken over for nonagricultural uses.

The Kenai Peninsula produces some beef, hay and potatoes. Kodiak Island produces more beef than any other area in the state.

The islands of Umnak and Unalaska graze 5,500 sheep for wool.

Based on Soil Conservation Service information, there are at least 15 million acres of potential farmland in Alaska suitable for raising crops, plus 108 million acres of range for livestock grazing, most of which is suitable only for reindeer.

Carrots, cabbage and other vegetables were also produced. They occasionally reach giant size because of the long daylight hours. Special varieties of cabbages up to 70 pounds and turnips over 30 pounds have been produced.

The Matanuska Valley produces 75% of the total crop sales, selling primarily to Anchorage and military markets. Dairy farming is the dominant income source, including feed crops for cows. The valley has a 120-day growing season that includes up to 19 hours of sunlight daily, warm temperatures and moderate rainfall. During most years, supplemental irrigation is required.

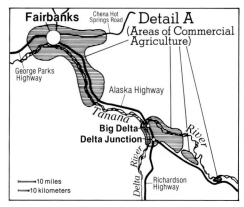

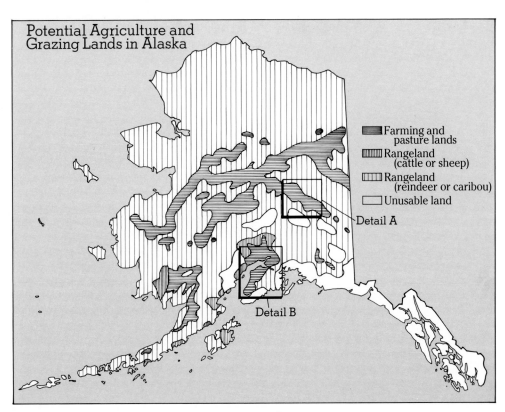

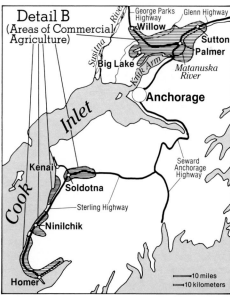

TRANSPORTATION

Air Travel

Alaska is the "flyingest" state in the Union; the only practical way to reach many areas of rural Alaska is by airplane. According to the Federal Aviation Administration, Alaskan Region, by the end of 1978 there were approximately 10,900 pilots—one out of every 39 Alaskans—and 6,800 registered aircraft—one for every 62 Alaskans. This figure is approximately six times as many pilots per capita and twelve times as many airplanes per capita as compared to the rest of the United States.

Lake Hood in Anchorage is the busiest seaplane base in the world. During peak summer and fall operating periods, more than 800 takeoffs and landings occur daily.

Merrill Field in Anchorage was the 20th busiest airport in the United States in 1978 (following Honolulu International Airport) with 365,213 takeoffs and landings recorded for the year.

Alaska has 513 airports and airstrips, 192 officially recognized seaplane landing sites and 41 heliports. In addition, there are numerous smaller, remote landing facilities and bush strips not designated on air navigational charts but used regularly by pilots.

For pilots who wish to fly their own planes to Alaska, a booklet titled *Flight Tips for Alaskan Tourists* may be obtained from the Federal Aviation Administration, 701 C Street, P.O. Box 14, Anchorage 99513.

In the spring of 1979, according to the Alaska Transportation Commission, 214 air taxi operations were in existence, as well as 9 contract carriers and 23 scheduled carriers.

INTERSTATE SERVICE—U.S. carriers providing interstate passenger service: Alaska Airlines, Northwest Orient Airlines, Western Airlines, Wien Air Alaska. These carriers and Flying Tigers provide freight service between Anchorage and Seattle. Reeve Aleutian Airways provides freight service between Cold Bay and Seattle.

Foreign carriers servicing Alaska through the Anchorage gateway: Air France, British Airways, Japan Air Lines, KLM Royal Dutch Airlines, Korean Airlines, Lufthansa German Airlines, Sabena-Belgian World Airlines, Scandinavian Airlines.

SERVICE WITHIN ALASKA—There is a long list of scheduled, and non-scheduled intrastate air carriers. Almost anywhere in Alaska, a charter aircraft is only a quick radio call away.

Highways

The state Department of Highways showed 6,833 miles of highways as of December 31, 1978, 6,719 rural miles (including 844 miles of ferry routes); 114.3 urban; 2,216 miles surfaced. At the present time the pipeline haul road from the Yukon River to Prudhoe Bay (350 miles) is not open to the public.

ALASKA HIGHWAY—The highway runs 1,520 miles through Canada and Alaska from Milepost 0 at Dawson Creek, British Columbia, to Fairbanks, Alaska. (The road from Milepost 1422 at Delta Junction to Fairbanks is sometimes considered part of the Richardson Highway.)

By agreement between the governments of Canada and the United States, the highway was built in 8 months by the U.S. Army Corps of Engineers and dedicated in November 1942. Crews worked south from Delta Junction, Alaska, north and south from Whitehorse, Yukon Territory, and north from Dawson Creek, British Columbia.

Two major sections of the highway were connected on September 23, 1942, at Contact Creek, Milepost 588.1, where the 35th Engineer Combat Regiment working west from Fort Nelson met the 340th Engineer General Service Regiment working east from Whitehorse. The last link in the highway was completed November 20, when the 97th Engineer General Service Regiment, heading east from Tanacross, met the 18th Engineer Combat Regiment at Milepost 1200.9, coming northwest from Kluane Lake. On this day a "pioneer" form of highway was completed. A

Alaska Mileage Chart

	Alaska Boundary	Anchorage	Chicago, IL	Circle	Dawson Creek, BC	Delta Junction	Eagle	Edmonton, AB	Fairbanks	Glennallen	Great Falls, MT	Haines	Haines Jct., YT	Homer	Livengood	Los Angeles, CA	New York, NY	Palmer	Paxson	Portage	Seattle, WA	Seward	Tok	Valdez	Whitehorse, YT
Alaska Boundary		421	3506	463	1221	201	242	1591	298	232	2106	364	205	648	380	3208	4347	373	274	469	2063	550	93	347	304
Anchorage	421		3927	523	1642	340	503	2012	358	189	2527	785	626	227	440	3629	4768	40	259	48	2484	129	328	304	725
Chicago, IL	3506	3927		3969	2285	3707	3748	1915	3804	3738	1400	3460	3301	4154	3886	2095	840	3879	3780	3975	2103	4056	3599	3853	3202
Circle	463	523	3969		1684	262	545	2054	165	413	2569	827	668	750	223	3671	4810	483	343	571	2526	652	370	528	767
Dawson Creek, BC	1221	1642	2285	1684		1422	1463	370	1519	1453	885	1175	1016	1869	1601	1987	3126	1594	1495	1690	842	1771	1314	1568	917
Delta Junction	201	340	3707	262	1422		283	1792	97	151	2307	565	406	567	179	3409	4548	292	81	388	2264	469	108	266	505
Eagle	242	503	3748	545	1463	283		1833	380	314	2348	606	447	730	462	3450	4589	455	356	551	2305	632	175	429	546
Edmonton, AB	1591	2012	1915	2054	370	1792	1833		1889	1823	515	1545	1386	2239	1971	2088	2756	1964	1865	2060	943	2141	1684	1938	1287
Fairbanks	298	358	3804	165	1519	97	380	1889		248	2404	662	503	585	82	3506	4645	389	178	406	2361	487	205	363	602
Glennallen	232	189	3738	413	1453	151	314	1823	248		2338	596	437	416	330	3440	4579	141	70	237	2295	318	139	115	536
Great Falls, MT	2106	2527	1400	2569	885	2307	2348	515	2404	2338		2060	1901	2754	2486	1848	2241	2479	2380	2575	703	2656	2199	2453	1802
Haines	364	785	3460	827	1175	565	606	1545	662	596	2060		159	1012	744	3162	4301	737	638	833	2017	914	457	711	258
Haines Jct., YT	205	626	3301	668	1016	406	447	1386	503	437	1901	159		853	585	3003	4142	578	479	674	1858	755	298	552	99
Homer	648	227	4154	750	1869	567	730	2239	585	416	2754	1012	853		667	3856	4995	267	486	179	2711	172	555	531	952
Livengood	380	440	3886	223	1601	179	462	1971	82	330	2486	744	585	667		3588	4727	400	260	488	2443	569	287	445	684
Los Angeles, CA	3208	3629	2095	3671	1987	3409	3450	2088	3506	3440	1848	3162	3003	3856	3588		2915	3581	3482	3677	1145	3758	3301	3555	2904
New York, NY	4347	4768	840	4810	3126	4548	4589	2756	4645	4579	2241	4301	4142	4995	4727	2915		4720	4621	4816	2944	4897	4440	4694	4043
Palmer	373	40	3879	483	1594	292	455	1964	389	141	2479	737	578	267	400	3581	4720		211	88	2436	169	280	256	677
Paxson	274	259	3780	343	1495	81	356	1865	178	70	2380	638	479	486	260	3482	4621	211		307	2337	388	181	185	578
Portage	469	48	3975	571	1690	388	551	2060	406	237	2575	833	674	179	488	3677	4816	88	307		2532	81	376	352	773
Seattle, WA	2063	2484	2103	2526	842	2264	2305	943	2361	2295	703	2017	1858	2711	2443	1145	2944	2436	2337	2532		2613	2156	2410	1759
Seward	550	129	4056	652	1771	469	632	2141	487	318	2656	914	755	172	569	3758	4897	169	388	81	2613		457	433	854
Tok	93	328	3599	370	1314	108	175	1684	205	139	2199	457	298	555	287	3301	4440	280	181	376	2156	457		254	397
Valdez	347	304	3853	528	1568	266	429	1938	363	115	2453	711	552	531	445	3555	4694	256	185	352	2410	433	254		651
Whitehorse, YT	304	725	3202	767	917	505	546	1287	602	536	1802	258	99	952	684	2904	4043	677	578	773	1759	854	397	651	

ceremony commemorating the event was held at Soldier Summit, approximately 100 miles east of the Alaska-Yukon border, and the first truck to negotiate the entire highway left that day from Soldier Summit and arrived in Fairbanks the next day.

The highway was built to relieve Alaska from the wartime hazards of shipping and to supply a land route for wartime materiel and equipment. It was then turned over to civilian contractors for widening and graveling, replacing log bridges with steel, and rerouting at many points. Today, the Alaska Highway is paved for its entire 298.7 miles within the state of Alaska, from Dawson Creek north 93 miles in British Columbia and for 23.9 miles near Whitehorse in Yukon Territory. The remaining 1,104.4 Canadian miles are gravel.

Driving the Alaska Highway requires a few preparations like protecting your car against gravel and carrying some spare parts. A partial list of spares includes: trailer bearings, fan belts, tires, jumper cables, siphoning hose, all-purpose plastic tape, wire, strong glue, selection of sheet-metal screws, rubber washers of various sizes, tire chains, tire pump, tire repair kit, tire breakdown tools, complete tool kit, points, condenser and spark plugs.

Preparation for gravel: Protect headlights with clear plastic covers made specifically for that purpose. In addition, you might consider a wire-mesh screen across the front of your vehicle to protect paint and radiator from flying rocks.

Substituting metal for rubber in the fuel lines underneath the car will provide longer wear. The rubber boots on axle joints of front-wheel-drive vehicles should be checked frequently. Rotating the tires every 1,000 miles or so will extend tire life.

There is practically no way to protect the windshield, although motorists have experimented with screen shields that do not seri-

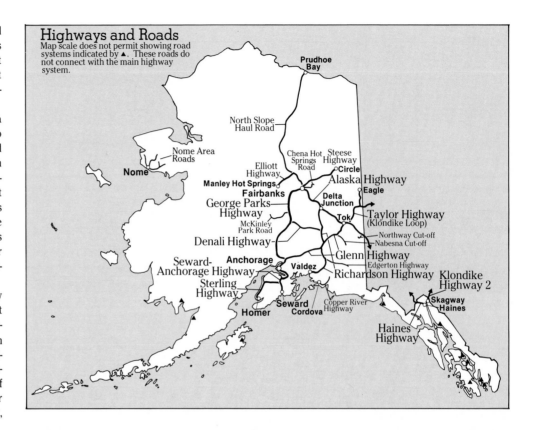

Highways and Roads
Map scale does not permit showing road systems indicated by ▲. These roads do not connect with the main highway system.

ously impair their vision. Larger towns throughout the Northland have auto-glass repair shops.

Gas tanks are often damaged. To protect them insert a rubber mat between gas tank and securing straps—old rubber mats and truck flaps work well.

If your car should break down on the highway and tow truck service is needed, normally you will be able to flag down a passing motorist. Travelers in the North are especially helpful in such situations and the etiquette of the country requires one to stop. If you are the only person traveling in the disabled car, be sure to leave a note on your windshield indi-

cating when you left the car and in what direction you planned to travel. This is particularly important when traveling in winter.

Dust protection: Along the Alaska Highway dust is at its worst following heavy rain and in construction areas. If you encounter much dust, check your air filter frequently. To help keep dust out of your vehicle, try to keep air pressure in the car by closing all windows and turning on the fan. Filtered heating and air-conditioning ducts in a vehicle bring in much less dust than open windows or vents. Mosquito netting placed over the heater/fresh air intake and flow-through ventilation will also help eliminate dust.

Railroads

The Alaska Railroad, operated by the Federal Railroad Administration of the U.S. Department of Transportation, provides passenger, vehicle, and freight service between Anchorage and Fairbanks, and Anchorage and Whittier. Passenger service is daily between mid-May and mid-September. In winter, twice-weekly service is available between Anchorage and Fairbanks. For information contact the Alaska Railroad, Pouch 7-2111, Anchorage 99510; phone 265-2685 for the Anchorage passenger agent or 265-2490 for the traffic division. In Fairbanks call 456-4155 for the passenger agent or 456-7736 for freight.

The privately owned White Pass & Yukon Route is a narrow-gauge link between Skagway, Alaska and Whitehorse, Yukon Territory. At the time it was built—1898 to 1900—it was the farthest north any railroad had operated in North America. It has one of the steepest railroad grades in North America, climbing to 2,885 at White Pass in only 20 miles of track. For information, contact the White Pass depot in either Skagway or Whitehorse; or write White Pass & Yukon Route, Box 2147, Seattle, Washington 98111.

Cruise Ships

At least eight privately operated cruise ship lines provide a luxurious means of seeing Southeastern Alaska. The ships depart from West Coast ports between June and September, following the Inside Passage on voyages that usually last five to seven days. One or two companies offer itineraries featuring open ocean travel to more northern Alaska ports. An estimated 75,000 cruise ship passengers visited Southeastern Alaska in 1978.

Additional information is available from the Alaska Division of Tourism, Pouch E, Juneau 99811.

Alaska State Ferries

The Alaska Marine Highway System operates the Southeastern and Southwestern Alaska ferry systems. There is NO service connecting the two systems.

Southwestern Alaska is served by two ferries. The *Bartlett* (193 feet) carries 165 passengers and provides service between Valdez, Cordova and Whittier. The *Tustumena* (296 feet) carries 200 passengers and serves Seward, Homer, Seldovia, Port Lions, Kodiak, Valdez, Cordova, King Cove and Sand Point. Service between Whittier and Valdez is via the Columbia Glacier and operates summers only. Also, service to King Cove and Sand Point is during the summer only.

The Alaska Marine Highway in Southeastern Alaska uses seven large vessels to move vehicles and people between 14 Southeastern Alaska ports, and also provides regularly scheduled service to and from Prince Rupert, British Columbia, and Seattle, Washington. The Southeastern ports of call are Ketchikan, Metlakatla, Hollis (access to Craig, Klawock and Thorne Bay), Wrangell, Petersburg, Kake, Sitka, Angoon, Pelican, Hoonah, Tenakee Springs, Juneau, Haines and Skagway.

The seven vessels of the Southeastern system are: the *Columbia* (418 feet, 650-1,000 passengers), *Chilkat* (99 feet, 75 passengers), *Malaspina* (408 feet, 600-750 passengers), *Matanuska* (408 feet, 600-750 passengers), *Taku* (352 feet, 500 passengers), *LeConte* (235 feet, 250 passengers) and the *Aurora* (235 feet, 250 passengers).

Reservations are required for vehicles and staterooms. They may be made through your travel agent or any Alaska Marine Highway terminal office; the main office is Alaska Marine Highway Systems, Pouch R, Juneau 99811, phone (907) 465-3941.

FLORA

WILD FLOWERS

Alaska's wild flowers are sometimes flamboyant; most commonly they are small and delicate. There are approximately 1,500 plant species in the state, including trees, shrubs, ferns, grasses and sedges.

Alpine regions are particularly rich in flora and some of the species are quite rare. Eagle Summit (Steese Highway), Thompson Pass (Richardson Highway), Maclaren Summit (Denali Highway), Polychrome Pass (McKinley Park), Turnagain Pass (Seward-Anchorage Highway) and Hatcher Pass (near Wasilla) are wonderful botanizing areas and are all easily accessible by car. There are, of course, many other regions to delight the wild flower fancier but they are more remote.

BERRIES

Edible wild berries are abundant in Alaska, with the lowbush cranberry, or lingonberry (*Vaccinium vitis-idaea*), being perhaps the most widespread of the approximately 50 species of wild berries found in the state. Wild strawberries, blueberries, raspberries, cloudberries, nagoonberries, salmonberries, crowberries, watermelon berries, currants and rose hips all ripen in summer and early fall.

POISONOUS PLANTS

There are poisonous plants in Alaska but not many considering the total quantity of plant species growing in the state. Baneberry (*Actaea rubra*), water hemlock (*Cicuta douglasii* and *C. mackenzieana*) and fly amanita mushroom (*Amanita muscarie*) are the most dangerous. Be sure you have properly identified plants before harvesting for food.

TREES

Thirty-three tree species grow in Alaska and only 12 of these reach 70 feet or more in height. Sitka spruce reach 225 feet in height and Western hemlock grow to 190 feet. Among the most common are the willow, spruce, poplar and alder. Four species in southeast Alaska are rare and are not likely to be seen without a special trip: Pacific yew, Pacific silver fir, subalpine fir and Hooker willow. (see also *Timber*, page 147.)

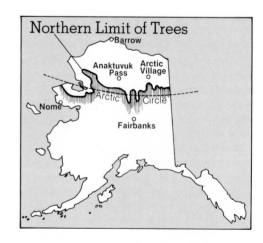

Northern Limit of Trees

FAUNA

MAMMALS

Large Land Mammals

Black bear—Found in most of Alaska. Absent from Southeastern islands north of Frederick Sound; not found west of about Naknek Lake on the Alaska Peninsula, in the Aleutian Islands or on the open tundra sloping into the Bering Sea and Arctic Ocean.

Brown/grizzly bear—Found in most of Alaska. Absent from Southeastern islands south of Frederick Sound and from the extreme Aleutians.

Polar bear—IT IS CURRENTLY ILLEGAL FOR ANYONE BUT AN ALASKAN ESKIMO, ALEUT OR INDIAN TO HUNT POLAR BEAR. There are two groups: a northern group found largely in the Beaufort Sea, and a western group found in the Chukchi Sea between Alaska and Siberia. The latter group are the largest polar bears in the world.

Bison—Four herds at Delta Junction, McGrath, Healy and in the Copper River drainage.

Caribou—Of the 13 herds, two are shared with Canada: Adak, Alaska Peninsula, Arctic, Beaver, Chisana, Delta, Kenai, McKinley, Mentasta, Mulchatna, Nelchina, Porcupine and Fortymile. The last two are shared.

Sitka blacktail deer—Coastal rain forests of Southeastern; expanded by transplants to Yakutat area, Prince William Sound and Kodiak and Afognak islands.

Elk—Transplanted in 1928 from Olympic Peninsula, Washington, to Raspberry and Afognak islands.

Moose—Found from the Stikine River in the Panhandle to the Colville River on the Arctic Slope. Most abundant in second-growth birch forests, on timber line plateaus and along major rivers of Southcentral and Interior.

Mountain goat—Most common within 50 miles of salt water from Southeastern north along the coast and on the Kenai Peninsula; transplanted to Kodiak; also found in the Alaska Range north and east of Cook Inlet.

Musk ox—Transplanted to Nunivak Island and from there to Barter Island area, near Nome, at Cape Thompson and on Nelson Island.

Dall sheep—Found in most of the high mountains except the Aleutian Range south of Iliamna Lake.

Wolf—Inhabits most of Alaska except Bering Sea Islands, some Southeastern and Prince William Sound Islands and the Aleutian Islands. Classified as big game and as fur bearer.

Wolverine—Found throughout Interior and the Arctic; on the full length of the Alaska Peninsula; much of Southeastern except some islands.

Fur Bearers

Fur animals that may be taken with a hunting license include coyote, blue or white arctic fox, red fox, lynx, red squirrel, wolf and wolverine. No hunting is allowed for beaver, marmot, marten, mink, weasel, muskrat, land and sea otter, and flying and ground squirrels. Animals are found in the following areas:

Beaver—Found along watercourses from Southeastern to the headwaters of the Kobuk and Selawik rivers in the Brooks Range; abundant in the Susitna, Kuskokwim and Yukon river drainages; plentiful on watersheds that drain into Bristol Bay; transplanted to Kodiak Island.

Coyote—Generally in the upper Tanana River Valley in the vicinity of Northway and southwest onto the Kenai Peninsula; a few in the Arctic and along the lower Yukon; recorded on the Southeastern mainland.

Arctic fox—White color phase found from the Kuskokwim River along the coast to Point Barrow and east along the Arctic Ocean coast into Canada and Greenland; on Nunivak, Hall, Saint Matthews, Saint Lawrence, Aleutian and Pribilof islands. Blue phase formerly raised commercially from Aleutians through Prince William Sound, outer Kenai Peninsula, to Southeastern.

Red fox—Most abundant from Unimak Island east to the base of the Alaska Peninsula, then north and east through the valleys of the Kuskokwim and Yukon rivers. Rare in Southeastern.

Lynx—Throughout the state except on the extreme Arctic Slope, the Aleutian Islands and islands of the Panhandle.

Marmot—Rocky slopes above timber line; occasionally at sea level along the Coast Mountains and on the Kenai Peninsula.

Marten—Mostly in thick spruce of the Alaska Range, the Brooks Range, along the headwaters of the Kuskokwim and in the Wrangell Mountains. Natural on Admiralty, Kuiu, Kupreanof and Revillagigedo islands and transplanted to Prince of Wales and Chichagof islands.

Mink—Throughout the state except the extreme north and in the Aleutian Islands; found along streams or the coast.

Muskrat—From Southeastern Panhandle north to the head of Kotzebue Sound; delta regions of Kobuk, Selawik, Yukon and Kuskokwim rivers; Yukon Flats.

Land (river) otter—Streams and lakes throughout most of the state, plus inland bays and tidal estuaries.

Sea otter—Aleutian Islands, Prince William Sound, lower Cook Inlet, Southeastern.

Flying squirrel—Forests from Southeastern north to the Arctic and mostly west of Fort Yukon.

Ground squirrel—Irregularly over the state north of the Gulf of Alaska.

Red squirrel—Throughout the forests of Southeastern, north of the edge of spruce forests.

Weasel—Throughout the state except the islands west of Umnak.

Other Small Mammals

Arctic hare—Tundra region of northern and northwestern Alaska; Yukon-Kuskokwim Delta; Bristol Bay area and west on the Alaska Peninsula.

Snowshoe hare—Wooded areas from Southeastern north to and beyond the limit of spruce trees.

Porcupine—Most wooded regions of mainland Alaska.

Marine Mammals

Marine mammals—whales, sea lions, seals phant), walrus and porpoises—MAY BE HUNTED ONLY BY AN ALASKAN ESKIMO, ALEUT OR INDIAN BY FEDERAL LAW. Elephant seals are protected by state regulations.

BIRDS

Authorities at the University of Alaska acknowledge 385 species of birds in Alaska; if undocumented sightings are included, the number of species increases to more than 400. Of the 385 species, 174 are permanent residents of Alaska; the others are migrants. Although only about half the species are waterfowl, they are by far the most numerous and important birds of the state. Millions upon millions of waterfowl make their way north each spring to take advantage of Alaska's lakes, tundra ponds and river flats. In addition, pelagic birds (seabirds) congregate in great nesting colonies on exposed sea cliffs along much of Alaska's coastline. Some of the best-known pelagic bird areas are in the Aleutian and Pribilof Islands.

Migratory birds gather in Alaska from many corners of the world. The Arctic tern travels up to 22,000 miles round trip each year from Antarctic waters to breed in Alaska. The wheatear makes its way to the state from Africa. The American golden plover nests in Alaska and winters in Hawaii. Other species travel between Alaska and Asia.

The Copper River Delta, situated along one of the most important migration routes in the state, is relatively accessible to birdwatchers via the Copper River Highway from Cordova. Each May, one of the world's largest concentrations of birdlife—primarily sandpipers and dunlins—funnel by the millions through the delta region. The delta is also an important waterfowl breeding area, containing the

world's only breeding population of dusky Canada geese. Approximately four-fifths of the world's population of trumpeter swans nest in Alaska and the delta area. Although the swans were once thought near extinction, 4,170 were counted in 1975.

Other important waterfowl nesting areas include the great delta between the mouths of the Yukon and Kuskokwim rivers, Yukon Flats, Innoko Flats and Minto Lakes. Additional gathering spots during migration include Egegik, Port Heiden, Port Moller, Izembek Bay, Chickaloon Flats, Susitna Flats and Stikine Flats. A few species of birds— including shearwaters, albatross and petrels— breed in Antarctic waters and winter in Alaska during the Northern Hemisphere's summer.

FISH AND SHELLFISH

Between 40 and 50 species of fish are found in Alaska's lakes and streams, and far more species and subspecies inhabit the thousands of miles of salt-water coastline of the state—several hundred, probably.

By far the most familiar fish in Alaska are the members of the salmon family—the salmon and trout—including the five species of Pacific salmon: King (sometimes called chinook, tyee or spring salmon); silver (also known as coho); red (often called sockeye); pink (or humpback); and chum (sometimes known as dog salmon).

All five species are important to commercial fishermen, and two of these—the king and silver—have long been regarded as among the top game fish of the world.

Included in the trout category are the rainbow trout, cutthroat, lake trout, Dolly Varden, arctic char and the eastern brook trout, all more-or-less related, with the same general appearance and characteristics.

Other common fresh-water species include: Arctic grayling, sheefish, great northern pike, fresh-water ling, whitefish and eulachon.

Some of the most common salt-water fish are: Pacific halibut, rockfish, sablefish, Pacific cod, Pacific tomcod, walleye pollock, sculpin, flounder, sole and dogfish.

Shellfish, which include crabs of various species, clams, shrimp and scallops, are abundant in Alaska. Common crab species include: king crab, Dungeness crab and tanner crab—the three favorites among commercial and sport fishermen. Shrimp are found in great abundance along the Alaskan coast—largest being the spot shrimp, which may be up to 18 inches in length. Others include the humpback, pink and coonstripe shrimp.

Of the many common species of clams found in Alaska—cockle, little neck, butter and many others—the favorite among diggers is the razor clam, excavated on minus tides of spring and fall from a few scattered beaches, primarily in Southcentral Alaska. The butter clam, however, has its strong supporters and is much more widely distributed from the Bering Sea to the Pacific Northwest.

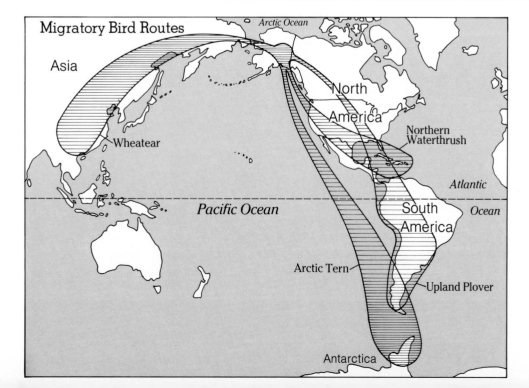

Migratory Bird Routes

Four species of endangered birds are found in Alaska: the Aleutian Canada goose, the peregrine falcon (Arctic and American races), the Eskimo curlew and the short-tailed albatross.

Three chapters of the National Audubon Society are based in Alaska: the Anchorage Audubon Society, Inc. (P.O. Box 1161, Anchorage 99510), the Juneau Audubon Society (P.O. Box 822, Juneau 99802) and the Arctic Audubon Society (P.O. Box 60524, Fairbanks 99701). In addition to trying to help people increase their knowledge of birds and their surroundings, the groups coordinate an annual Christmas bird count.

FACTS ABOUT ALASKA

ARCTIC CIRCLE

The Arctic Circle is the latitude at which the sun does not set for one day at midsummer and does not rise for one day at midwinter, when the sun is at its greatest distance from the celestial equator. The latitude, which varies slightly from year to year, is approximately 66°33′ from the equator.

On the day of summer solstice, on June 20 or 21, the sun does not set at the Arctic Circle; because of refraction of sunlight, it appears not to set for 4 days. Farther north, at Barrow (northernmost community in the United States), the sun does not set from May 10 to August 2.

At winter solstice, December 21 or 22, the sun does not rise for 1 day at the Arctic Circle. At Barrow, it does not rise for 67 days.

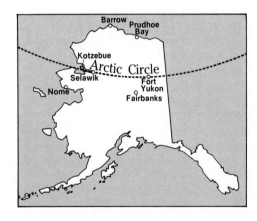

AURORA BOREALIS

The aurora borealis is produced by gas particles in the upper atmosphere being struck by solar electronics trapped in the earth's magnetic field. Color varies depending on how hard the gas particles are being struck and range from simple arcs to drapery-like forms in green, red, blue and purple. The lights occur in a pattern rather than as a solid glow because electric current sheets flowing through gases create V-shaped potential double layers. Electrons near the center of the current sheet move faster, hit the atmosphere harder, and cause the different intensities of light observed in the aurora.

Displays occur about 68 miles above the earth's surface, concentrated in two bands roughly centered above the Arctic Circle and Antarctic Circle. Greatest occurrence of auroral displays is in the spring and fall months, although displays may occur on dark nights throughout the winter.

Some observers claim the northern lights make a noise similar to the rustle of taffeta, but scientists say the displays cannot be heard in the audible frequency range.

To capture the northern lights on film, you will need a sturdy tripod, a locking-type cable release (some 35mm cameras have both *time* and *bulb* settings, but most have *bulb only,* which calls for use of the locking-type cable release), and a camera with a f/3.5 lens (or faster).

It is best to photograph the lights on a night when they are not moving too rapidly. And, as a general rule, photos improve if you manage to include recognizable subjects in the foreground—trees and lighted cabins being favorites of many photographers. Set your camera up at least 75 feet back from the foreground objects to make sure that both the foreground and aurora are in sharp focus.

Normal and wide-angle lenses are best. Try to keep your exposures under a minute—10 to 30 seconds are generally best. The following lens openings and exposure times are only a starting point, since the amount of light generated by the aurora is inconsistent. (It's best to bracket exposures widely for best results.)

	ASA 200	ASA 400
f1.2	3 sec.	2 sec.
f1.4	5	3
f1.8	7	4
f2	20	10
f2.8	40	20
f3.5	60	30

Ektachrome 200 and 400 color films can be push-processed in the home darkroom or by some custom-color labs, allowing use of higher ASA ratings (800, 1200 or even 1600 on the 400 ASA film, for example). Kodak will push-process film if you include an ESP-1 envelope with your standard film-processing mailer. (Consult your local camera store for details.)

A few notes of caution:

Protect the camera from low temperatures until you are ready to make your exposures. Some newer cameras, in particular, have electrically controlled shutters that will not function properly at low temperatures.

Wind the film slowly to reduce the possibility of static electricity, which can lead to streaks on the film. Grounding the camera when rewinding can help prevent the static-electricity problem. (To ground the camera, hold it against a water pipe, drain pipe, metal fence post or other grounded object.)

Follow the basic rules, experiment with exposures, and you should obtain good results.

BALEEN

Baleen is a hornlike fringed substance that lines the mouth of certain species of whales. Baleen strains out plankton, the tiny, shrimp-like creatures called krill and small fish from the water. Once used for corset stays and buggy whips, baleen is no longer used commercially, although Alaska Natives still use brownish black bowhead baleen to make baskets and small boats for the tourist trade.

BARABARA

Pronounced *buh-rah-buh-rah*, this traditional Aleut or Eskimo shelter is built of sod supported by driftwood or whalebone.

BOATING

With Alaska's lack of highways, travel by boat is an important means of transportation to otherwise inaccessible areas. Until the advent of the airplane, boats were often the only way to reach many areas of Alaska. Most of Alaska's supplies still arrive by water, and in Southeastern Alaska, where precipitous terrain and numerous islands make roads extremely expensive and bad weather makes airplane travel often unreliable, water travel is essential to existence.

More and more, people are discovering the pleasures of motorboating, sailing, canoeing, rafting, kayaking and powering shallow-draft riverboats through Alaska's vast water wilderness.

Alaska's thousands of lakes, for example, provide nearly endless exploration possibilities. Southwest Alaska in particular, with Wood Tikchik State Park, Katmai National Monument, Lake Iliamna and Lake Clark, is a region of large, clear lakes. Canoeists in Southcentral Alaska find well-traveled, road-accessible routes in the Kenai National Moose Range (P.O. Box 500, Kenai 99611) and in Nancy Lake Recreation Area (Alaska Division of Parks, Mat-Su District, P.O. Box 182, Palmer 99645).

River travel opportunities, in both calm water and whitewater, are too numerous and varied to mention here. Alaska's salt-water cruising areas have been proclaimed by experienced boaters to be among the best in the world. Alaska's shoreline offers protected, island-dotted, lagoon-lined passages ideal for kayaking, fjords headed by restless tidewater glaciers, and storm-whipped sandy ocean beaches. Wildlife and excellent fishing enhance the spectacular scenery.

Travel by water in Alaska requires extra caution, however. Weather changes fast and is often unpredictable; it's important to be prepared for the worst. Alaska waters, even in midsummer, are cold; a person falling overboard may become immobilized by the cold water in only a few minutes. And since on many of Alaska's water routes one is so remote from civilization, help may be a long way off.

Persons inexperienced in traveling Alaska's waterways might consider employing a charter boat operator or outfitter. Guides offer local knowledge and provide all necessary equipment. The Division of Tourism (Pouch E, Juneau 99811) maintains current lists of such services. Another place to find names of guides and charter skippers is in The Guide Post® in *ALASKA*® magazine, available from Alaska Northwest Publishing Company.

CAMPING

Numerous public and privately operated campgrounds are found along Alaska's highways. Electrical hookups and dumping stations are scarce. Alaska's back country offers virtually limitless possibilities for wilderness camping. Get permission before camping on private land. If the land is publicly owned, it's worthwhile to contact the agency that manages the land regarding regulations and hiking/camping conditions. Additional details about camping are found in *The MILEPOST*®.

THE U.S. FOREST SERVICE maintains campgrounds in the Tongass (Southeastern Alaska) and Chugach (eastern Kenai Peninsula and Prince William Sound) national forests. A campsite usually accommodates a tent, although some take trailers. All campgrounds are available first-come-first-served and there is usually a $1 to $2 fee per night. Campgrounds are open from June through September. (See also *Forest Service Cabins.*)

THE NATIONAL PARK SERVICE (State office: 540 West Fifth Avenue, Anchorage 99501) at Mount McKinley National Park offers seven campgrounds accessible by road. Situated near the park entrance and open year round, Riley Creek, for vehicles, and Morino, for walk-in campers, are open on a first-come, first-served basis. The others, open between

May and September, depending on weather conditions, must be reserved upon arrival at the park. Reservations may be made for up to 14 days. No fee is charged for primitive campgrounds. Teklanika River Campground costs $2 per night; Riley Creek, Savage River and Wonder Lake cost $4 per night. Brochures may be obtained from Mount McKinley National Park, P.O. Box 9, Mount McKinley 99755.

Glacier Bay National Monument and Katmai National Monument each offer one campground for walk-in campers. Back-country camping is permitted in McKinley, Glacier Bay, Katmai and Klondike Gold Rush National Historical Parks and the national monuments declared in 1978.

ALASKA DIVISION OF PARKS (619 Warehouse Avenue, Suite 210, Anchorage 99501) maintains the most extensive system of roadside campgrounds and waysides in Alaska. No fees are charged. (See *State Park System*.)

THE FEDERAL BUREAU OF LAND MANAGEMENT (Fairbanks District Office, P.O. Box 1150, Fairbanks 99707) maintains 27 campgrounds in Interior Alaska. The campground at Delta Junction has a fee of $2 per night; all other BLM campgrounds are free. Brochures describing the campgrounds are available from the above address or from the state office, 701 C Street, P.O. Box 13, Anchorage 99513.

U.S. FISH & WILDLIFE SERVICE (state office: 1011 East Tudor, Anchorage 99504; Kenai National Moose Range, P.O. Box 500, Kenai 99611) has sites available to campers. With the exception of a few bird refuges easily disrupted by human presence, back-country camping is permitted in wildlife refuges. There are no fees and few restrictions. Temporary structures may be erected for a maximum of 60 days. Kenai National Moose Range, on the northwestern Kenai Peninsula, has 19 campgrounds and 14 waysides. No fees are charged. Contact local refuge managers for up-to-date information. (See *National Wildlife Refuges and Ranges*.)

COST OF LIVING

Cost of various items — food, clothing, housing, gasoline are generally higher in Alaska and Canada than in the Lower 48. To give visitors a rough idea of what to expect, we have compiled the following list of costs (U.S. dollars) in Juneau, Anchorage and Whitehorse, YT. At press time U.S. dollars were more than Canadian — exchange rate was approximately 18%. Prices were sampled in late 1979.

	JUNEAU	ANCHORAGE	WHITEHORSE
Apartment rental, 2-bedroom	$225-$525*	$200-$500*	$300-$500*
Purchase 2-bedroom home	$55,000-$68,000*	$65,000-$90,000	$60,000-$90,000*
Purchase 3-bedroom home	$61,000-$75000*	$85,000-$95,000*	$60,000-$90,000*
Hotel room, double	$30-$55*	$45-$65*	$32-$58*
Gasoline, regular, per gal.	$1.03	$1.09-$1.12	$1.25-$1.50**
Gasoline, premium or unleaded, per gal.	$1.08	$1.10-$1.18	$1.30-$1.65**
Laundromat wash, normal load	$ .75	$ .75	$1
Laundromat dry, for 10 minutes	$ .20	$ .25	$ .25
Men's haircut (not styled)	$7.50-$10	$9	$7-$16
Woman's cut, shampoo, set	$12-$18	$20	$14-$20
Firewood per cord	$45-$75	$65-$90	$55-$80
Deluxe hamburger	$1.35-$3.50	$1.25-$3.75	$1.50-$2.50
Steak dinner (New York cut)	$12-$16	$12-$18	$10-$15
Cup of coffee	$ .25-$ .75	$ .35-$1	$ .25-$1.50
Beer, per case	$7-$12.50	$8-$12	$6
Bourbon, fith	$6.50-$11.50	$9-$11	$7-$12
Groceries—top brands			
Butter (1 lb.)	$1.55	$1.95	$1.50
Chicken fryer, per lb.	$1.10	$1.06	$1.10
Cola (6 pak)	$2.15	$2-$2.20	$2.10
Flour (10-lb. bag)	$2.70	$2.85	$2.65
Ground round, per lb.	$1.65	$1.98	$1.60
Milk (½ gal. 2%)	$1.45	$1.39	$1.45**
Oleomargarine (1 lb.)	$ .86	$1.25	$1.15
Orange juice (6 oz. frozen)	$ .65	$ .65	$ .53
Sirloin tip steak, per lb.	$4.45	$2.99	$4.45
Tuna (6½-oz. can)	$1.30	$1.12	$1.20

*and up   **Imperial gallon, about 20% larger than U.S. gallon

DAYLIGHT HOURS

Summer Maximum

	SUNRISE	SUNSET	LENGTH
Barrow	May 10	August 2	84 days
Fairbanks	12:59 a.m.	10:48 p.m.	21:49 hours
Anchorage	2:21 a.m.	9:42 p.m.	19:21 hours
Juneau	3:51 a.m.	10:09 p.m.	18:18 hours
Ketchikan	4:04 a.m.	9:33 p.m.	17:29 hours
Adak	5:27 a.m.	10:10 p.m.	16:43 hours

Winter Minimum

	SUNRISE	SUNSET	LENGTH
Barrow	Jan. 24 noon	Nov. 18 noon	67 days
Fairbanks	9:59 a.m.	1:41 p.m.	3:42 hours
Anchorage	9:14 a.m.	2:42 p.m.	5:28 hours
Juneau	9:46 a.m.	4:07 p.m.	6:21 hours
Ketchikan	9:12 a.m.	4:18 p.m.	7:06 hours
Adak	9:52 a.m.	5:38 p.m.	7:46 hours

DOG MUSHING

Sled dog racing is popular throughout the winter in Alaska with major races held during early spring. The World Championship Sled Dog Race is run during the Fur Rendezvous in Anchorage about the third weekend in February. Then comes the 1,049-mile Iditarod Trail Sled Dog Race from Anchorage to Nome, which begins the first weekend in March. The North American Sled Dog Championship in Fairbanks begins usually the third weekend in March. Other major races are held at Soldotna, Tok, Valdez, Bethel and Kotzebue, in addition to racing every weekend sponsored by various sled dog organizations around the state.

The sprint or championship races are usually run over two or three days with the cumulative time for the heats deciding the winner. Distances for the heats vary from 12 miles to 30 miles. The Iditarod, a difficult test for dog and musher, takes the teams north from Anchorage to the Yukon River, then west to the Bering Sea, turning north again to reach Nome on the Seward Peninsula. The record for the race is 14 days, 7 hours, 11 minutes and 51 seconds set in 1980 by Joe May of Trapper Creek. Rick Swenson became the first musher to win the Iditarod twice in 1979.

Purses range from trophies for the club races to $5,000 or $6,000, including heat money, for the championships, and as much as $14,500 for the winner of the Iditarod.

EARTHQUAKES

Between 1899 and May 1965 nine Alaska earthquakes occurred that equaled or exceeded a magnitude of 8 on the Richter scale. During the same period, more than 60 earthquakes took place that were of magnitude 7 or greater on the Richter scale.

According to the University of Alaska's Geophysical Institute, earthquake activity in Alaska typically follows the same pattern from month to month, interspersed with sporadic swarms, or groups of small earthquakes. The most active part of the state seismically is the Aleutian Island arc system. Seismicity related to this system extends into Interior Alaska to a point near Mount McKinley. These earthquakes are largely the result of underthrusting of the North Pacific plate and are characteristically deeper in the earth than most earthquakes. The majority of earthquakes resulting from this underthrusting occur in Cook Inlet—particularly near Mount Iliamna and Mount Redoubt—and near Mount McKinley. North of the Alaska Range, in the central Interior, most earthquakes are of shallow origin.

An earthquake created the highest splash wave ever recorded when, on the evening of July 10, 1958, a quake with a magnitude of 8 on the Richter scale rocked the Yakutat area. A landslide containing approximately 40 million cubic yards of rock plunged into Gilbert Inlet at the head of Lituya Bay. The gigantic splash resulting from the slide sent a wave 1,740 feet up the opposite mountainside, denuding it of trees and soil down to bedrock. It then fell back and swept through the length of the bay and out to sea. One fishing boat anchored in Lituya Bay at the time was lost with its crew of two; another was carried over a spit of land by the wave and soon after foundered, but its crew was saved. A third boat anchored in the bay miraculously survived intact. A total of four square miles of coniferous forest was destroyed.

The most destructive earthquake to strike Alaska took place at 5:36 P.M. March 27, 1964. Registering between 8.4 and 8.6 on the Richter scale, the earthquake was the strongest ever recorded in North America. With its primary epicenter deep beneath Miners Lake in Northern Prince William Sound, the earthquake spread shock waves over a 500-mile-wide area. The earthquake and seismic waves that followed killed 131 persons, 115 of them Alaskans. The death tally in the following communities was: Anchorage, 9; Chenega, 23; Kodiak, 19; Point Nowell, 1; Point Whitshed, 1; Port Ashton, 1; Port Nellie Juan, 3; Seward, 13; Valdez, 31; Whittier, 13. The earthquake released twice the energy of the San Francisco earthquake of 1906 and moved more earth farther, both horizontally and vertically, than any other earthquake ever recorded. In the 69-day period after the main quake, there were 12,000 jolts of 3.5 magnitude or greater.

The highest seismic sea wave ever recorded was caused by the 1964 earthquake when an undersea slide near Shoup Glacier in Port Valdez triggered a wave that toppled trees 100 feet above tidewater and deposited silt and sand 220 feet above salt water.

FIRES, FOREST AND TUNDRA

CALENDAR YEAR	NO. OF FIRES	ACRES BURNED
1955	190	23,582
1956	226	476,593
1957	391	5,049,661
1958	278	317,215
1959	320	596,574
1960	238	87,180
1961	117	5,100
1962	102	38,975
1963	194	16,290
1964	164	3,430
1965	148	7,093
1966	256	672,765
1967	207	109,005
1968	442	1,013,301
1969	511	4,231,820
1970	487	113,486
1971	472	1,069,108
1972	641	963,686
1973	336	59,816
1974	782	662,960
1975	344	127,845
1976	622	69,119
1977	681	2,290,408
1978	356	7,757

The largest single fire ever recorded in Alaska burned 1,161,200 acres 74 miles northwest of Galena in 1957, according to Bureau of Land Management figures. In 1977, the Bear Creek fire, largest in the United States that year, consumed 361,000 acres near the Farewell airstrip. During that same fire season, BLM logged 24,000 flying hours and smoke jumpers made a record 1,795 jumps.

FLAG

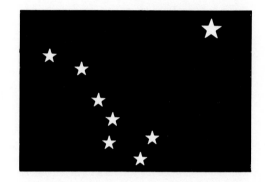

Alaska's state flag was designed by the late Benny Benson, winner of the territorial flag contest for schoolchildren in 1926, and adopted by the legislature on May 2, 1927. The flag consists of eight gold stars on a field of blue—the Big Dipper and the North Star. In Benson's words: "The blue field is for the Alaska sky and the forget-me-not, an Alaska flower. The North Star is for the future state of Alaska, the most northerly of the Union. The dipper is for the Great Bear—symbolizing strength."

Benny Benson was born October 12, 1913, at Chignik, Alaska. His mother was of Aleut-Russian descent and his father was a Swedish fisherman who came to the Alaska Territory in 1904.

When Benny was four, his mother died of pneumonia. Benny then entered the Jesse Lee Memorial Home, which was then located at Unalaska in the Aleutian Islands; it was later moved to Seward.

When he was 13, Benny entered a design in the Territorial flag contest which was open to all Alaska schoolchildren in grades seven through twelve. Benny, then a seventh grade student at the Jesse Lee Home, was one of 142 students whose designs were selected for the final judging by a committee chosen by the Alaska Department of the American Legion.

On May 2, 1927, the Alaska Legislature adopted the design as the official flag for the Territory of Alaska. Benny was awarded a scholarship and was presented with a watch for winning the contest. He used the scholarship to learn about diesel engines in a school in Seattle, Washington.

Benny's prophetic words, "The North Star is for the future state of Alaska, the most northerly of the Union," were realized on January 3, 1959 when Alaska was proclaimed the 49th State of the Union. The drafters of the Constitution for Alaska stipulated that the flag of the territory would be the official flag of the State of Alaska, and when the flag was first flown over the capital city on July 4, 1959, Benny proudly led the parade that preceded the ceremony, carrying the flag of "eight stars on a field of blue," which he had designed many years before.

On November 5, 1963, Benny presented the award watch to the Alaska State Museum.

Benny Benson lived in Kodiak for a number of years where he was an airplane mechanic. He died on July 2, 1972.

GOLD NUGGETS

The largest gold nugget ever found in Alaska was discovered near Nome. The nugget, weighing 107 ounces, 2 pennyweight, was found September 29, 1901, on Discovery Claim, Anvil Creek, Nome District. The nugget was 7 inches long, 4 inches wide and 2 inches thick.

Two other record-breaking nuggets were found in the Nome area the same month. On September 5, the largest Alaska nugget found up to that time was discovered on the Jarvis Brothers' claim on Anvil Creek. It weighed 45 ounces, and was 6¼ inches long, 3¼ inches wide, 1⅜ inches thick at one end and ½ inch thick at the other. On September 14, a larger nugget was found on the Discovery Claim; it weighed 97 ounces and broke the record of September 5 only to be superseded by the 107-ounce nugget found on the 29th.

GOLD STRIKES AND RUSHES

1848	First Alaska gold discovery (Russian on Kenai Peninsula)
1861	Stikine River near Telegraph Creek, British Columbia
1872	Cassiar district in Canada (Stikine headwaters country)
1872	Near Sitka
1874	Windham Bay near Juneau
1880	Gold Creek at Juneau
1886	Fortymile discovery
1887	Yakutat beach areas and Lituya Bay
1893	Mastodon Creek, starting Circle City
1895	Sunrise district on Kenai Peninsula
1896	Klondike strike, Bonanza Creek, Canada
1898	Anvil Creek, Nome
1900	Porcupine rush out of Haines
1902	Fairbanks (Felix Pedro, Pedro Dome)
1906	Innoko
1907	Ruby
1909	Iditarod
1913	Marshall
1913	Chisana
1914	Livengood

(See also *History*.)

FOREST SERVICE CABINS

U.S. Forest Service cabins in Alaska are available for $5 per night. Advance reservations, which may be made up to 180 days ahead of time, are mandatory, and you must have the necessary permit for the specific days you will be using the cabins. Unauthorized occupancy is a violation of both state and federal laws. The approximately 150 wilderness cabins, accessible mostly by air, are scattered throughout the Tongass and Chugach National Forests. To reserve the cabins write to the U.S. Forest Service, Tongass National Forest, Juneau 99802, or Chugach National Forest, Pouch 6606, Anchorage 99502; include full payment. It's also possible to stop by the Forest Service offices in Anchorage, Cordova, Juneau, Ketchikan, Kodiak, Petersburg, Seward, Wrangell and Yakutat, and rent a cabin in person.

Each cabin has a table, bunks and stove, but no plumbing, electricity, oil, cooking utensils, pillows or mattresses.

GOVERNORS OF ALASKA

Under Russia

Alexander Andreevich Baranov	1790-1818
Leontil Andreanovich Hagemeister	Jan.-Oct. 1818
Semen Ivanovich Yanovski	1818-1820
Matxei I. Muravief	1820-1825
Peter Egorovich Chistiakov	1825-1830
Baron Ferdinand P. von Wrangell	1830-1835
Ivan Antonovich Kupreanof	1835-1840
Adolph Karlovich Etolin	1840-1845
Michael D. Tebenkof	1845-1850
Nikolai Y. Rosenberg	1850-1853
Alexander Ilich Rudakof	1853-1854
Stephen Vasili Voevodski	1854-1859
Ivan V. Furuhelm	1859-1863
Prince Dmitri Maksoutoff	1863-1867

After the Purchase

Brevet Major Gen. Jeff C. Davis	Oct. 18, 1867-Dec. 1, 1868
Capt. W.H. Dennison (U.S. Army)	Dec. 1, 1868-July 3, 1869
Capt. G.K. Brady (U.S. Army)	July 3, 1869-Sept. 23, 1870
Maj. J.C. Tidball	Sept. 23, 1870-

U.S. troops were withdrawn in 1877, leaving M.C. Berry, customs collector, the only federal official in Alaska.

Capt. L.S. Beardslee (U.S. Navy), Sloop *Jamestown*	Apr. 1879-Oct. 1880
Henry Glass (U.S. Navy), assumed command from Beardslee	1880-
Edward P. Lull (U.S. Navy), the *Wachusett*	1880-1881
Lt. Comm. Henry E. Nichols (U.S. Navy), the *Pinta*	1884-1886

Presidential Appointments

John H. Kinkead (Pres. Arthur)	July 4, 1884-May 7, 1885
Alfred P. Swineford (Pres. Cleveland)	May 7, 1885-Apr. 20, 1889
Lyman E. Knapp (Pres. Harrison)	Apr. 20, 1889-June 18, 1893
James Sheakley (Pres. Cleveland)	June 18, 1893-June 23, 1897
John G. Brady (Pres. Roosevelt)	June 23, 1897-Mar. 2, 1906
Wilford B. Hoggatt (Pres. Roosevelt)	Mar. 2, 1906-May 20, 1909
Walter E. Clark (Pres. Taft)	May 20, 1909-Apr. 18, 1913
John F.A. Strong (Pres. Wilson)	Apr. 18, 1913-Apr. 12, 1918
Thomas Riggs Jr. (Pres. Wilson)	Apr. 12, 1918-June 16, 1921
Scott C. Bone (Pres. Harding)	June 16, 1921-Aug. 16, 1925

Presidential Appointments (continued)

George A. Parks (Pres. Coolidge)	June 16, 1925-Apr. 19, 1933
John W. Troy (Pres. Roosevelt)	Apr. 19, 1933-Dec. 6, 1939
Ernest Gruening (Pres. Roosevelt)	Dec. 6, 1939-Apr. 10, 1953
B. Frank Heintzleman (Pres. Eisenhower)	Apr. 10, 1953-Jan. 3, 1957
Mike Stepovich (Pres. Eisenhower)	Apr. 8, 1957-Aug. 9, 1958
SINCE STATEHOOD	
William A. Egan (Elected)	Jan. 3, 1959-Dec. 5, 1966
Walter J. Hickel (Elected—resigned)	Dec. 5, 1966-Jan. 29, 1969
Keith H. Miller (Succeeded)	Jan. 29, 1969-Dec. 5, 1970
William Egan (Elected)	Dec. 5, 1970-Dec. 5, 1974
Jay Hammond (Elected)	Dec. 5, 1974-

———— * * * * * * * * ————

Delegates to Congress

In 1906, Congress authorized Alaska to send a voteless delegate to the House of Representatives.

Frank H. Waskey	1906-1907
Thomas Cale	1907-1909
James Wickersham	1909-1917
Charles A. Sulzer	1917-contested election
James Wickersham	1918-seated as delegate
Charles A. Sulzer	1919-elected; died before taking office
George Grigsby	1919-elected in a special election
James Wickersham	1921-seated as delegate, having contested election of Grigsby
Dan A. Sutherland	1921-1930
James Wickersham	1931-1933
Anthony J. Dimond	1933-1944
E.L. Bartlett	1944-1958

Tennessee Plan Delegation:

Senators:		Representative:	
Ernest Gruening	1956-1958	Ralph Rivers	1956-1958
William Egan	1956-1958		
SINCE STATEHOOD			
Senators:		Representatives:	
E.L. Bartlett	1959-1968	Ralph Rivers	1959-1966
Ernest Gruening	1959-1968	Howard Pollock	1966-1970
Mike Gravel	1968-	Nicholas Begich	1970-1972
Ted Stevens	1968-	Don Young	1973-

HIKING

A variety of hiking trails for all levels of ability may be found in the state. If the hiker is experienced and has the proper topographic maps, some of the best Alaska hiking is cross-country above treeline. Using both maps and tide tables, it is also feasible to hike along ocean shorelines at low tide.

Hikers in Alaska must plan for rapidly-changing, inclement weather. Take raingear. If staying overnight in the backcountry, it's wise to carry a tent if a cabin is unavailable. Above treeline, snow can be encountered at any time of year.

Sporting goods stores in Alaska feature an excellent selection of hiking equipment. In addition, backcountry guides often furnish equipment on escorted expeditions.

Information on hiking in Alaska's national parks and monuments is available from the state office of the National Park Service, 540 West Fifth Avenue, Anchorage 99501, or from park headquarters for the area you're interested in. (See *National Forests, Parks and Monuments.*)

The Bureau of Land Management (office, 701 C Street, P.O. Box 13, Anchorage 99513) has brochures on the White Mountain Trail System and the Pinnell Mountain Trail.

The Alaska Division of Parks (see *State Park System*) has information on hiking on the lands managed by that agency.

The U.S. Fish and Wildlife Service (see *National Wildlife Refuges and Ranges*) offers some backcountry information on the areas they administer.

The U.S. Forest Service (see *National Forests, Parks and Monuments*) offers information on backcountry travel in the Chugach (Prince William Sound and western Kenai Peninsula) and Tongass (Southeast Alaska) national forests. The Forest Service maintains extensive trail networks in both these areas.

HISTORY

Numbers refer to accompanying map on page 170.

6,000-11,000 years ago—Human culture in Southeastern, Aleutians, Interior, and northwest Arctic Alaska.

6,000 years ago—Most recent migration from Siberia across the land bridge (1).

3,000-5,000 years ago—Human culture on the Bering Sea coast.

200-300 years ago—Tlingits and Haidas arrive.

1725—Vitus Bering sent by Peter the Great to explore the North Pacific.

1741—On a later expedition, Bering in one ship and Alexei Chirikof in another discover Alaska. Chirikof, according to ship logs, probably sees land on July 15 a day ahead of his leader, who was perhaps 300 miles or more to the north of him. Georg Steller goes ashore on Kayak Island, becoming the first white man known to have set foot on Alaskan soil (2).

1743—Concentrated hunting of sea otter begins, continuing until the species is almost decimated; fur seal hunting begins later.

1774-1794—Explorations of Alaskan waters by Juan Perez, James Cook (3) and George Vancouver.

1784—First Russian settlement in Alaska, at Three Saints Bay, Kodiak Island (4).

1786—Russians discover the Pribilof Islands (5), later to resettle Aleuts to the formerly uninhabited islands for fur sealing.

1794—Vancouver sights Mount McKinley.

1799—Alexander Baranof establishes the Russian post known today as Old Sitka (6); a trade charter is granted to the Russian-American Co.

1821—Russian-American Company given exclusive trading rights; no foreigners allowed in Russian America.

1824-1842—Russian exploration of the mainland leads to discovery of the Kuskokwim, Nushagak, Yukon and Koyukuk rivers.

1847—Fort Yukon established by Hudson's Bay Company (7).

1848—First mining in Alaska, on the Kenai Peninsula.

1853—Russian explorers-trappers find the first oil seeps in Cook Inlet.

1857—Coal mining begins at Coal Harbor, Kenai Peninsula, to supply steamers.

1859—Baron Edoard de Stoeckl, minister and charge d'affaires of the Russian delegation to the United States, is given authority to negotiate the sale of Alaska.

1867—United States buys Alaska from Russia for $7.2 million; fur seal population begins to stabilize. U.S. Army is given jurisdiction over the Department of Alaska the following year.

1872—Gold discovered near Sitka (6). Later discoveries include Juneau, 1876, 1880 (8); Fortymile, 1886 (9); Circle City, 1893 (10); Hope-Sunrise, 1896 (11); Klondike, 1896 (12); Nome, 1989 (13); Fairbanks, 1902 (14); Innoko, 1906 (15); Ruby, 1907 (16); Iditarod, 1908 (17); Marshall, 1913 (18); Chisana, 1913 (19); and Livengood, 1914 (20).

1878—First salmon canneries at Klawock and Old Sitka.

1887—Tsimshians, under Father William Duncan, arrived at Metlakatla from British Columbia.

1891—First Siberian reindeer brought to Unalaska by Sheldon Jackson (21).

1891—First oil claims staked in Cook Inlet area.

1897-1900—Klondike gold rush in Yukon; heavy traffic through Alaska.

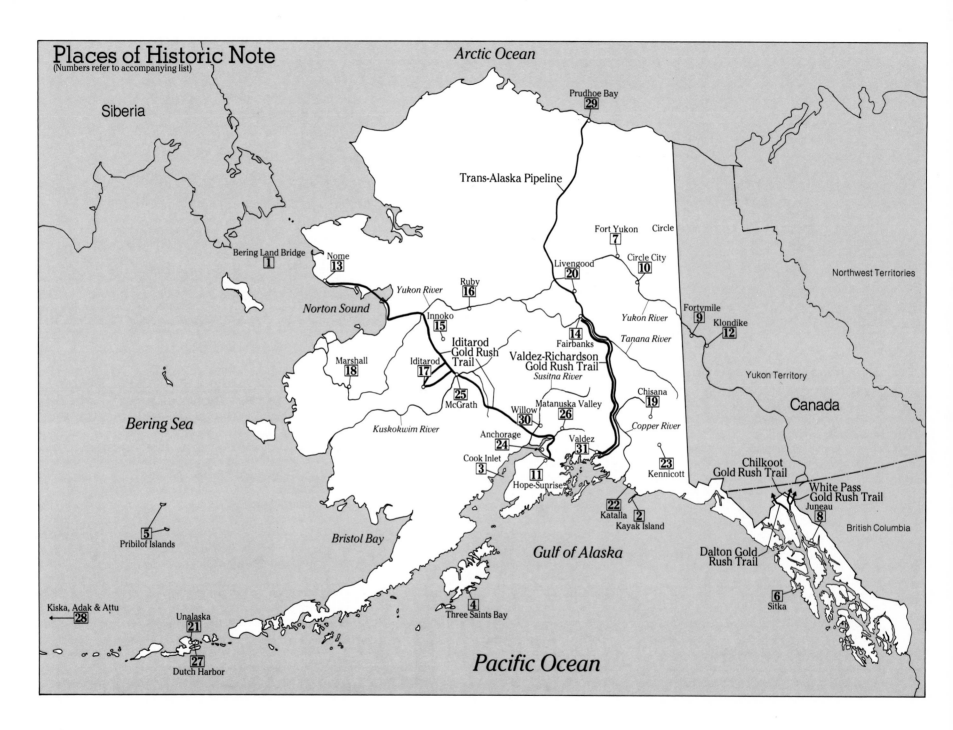

Places of Historic Note

(Numbers refer to accompanying list)

Arctic Ocean

Siberia

Prudhoe Bay **29**

Trans-Alaska Pipeline

Fort Yukon **7**   Circle

Bering Land Bridge **1**   Nome **13**

Livengood **20**   Circle City **10**

Norton Sound   Ruby **16**   *Yukon River*

Fortymile **9**   Klondike **12**

Yukon River   Innoko **15**   **14**   *Tanana River*   Yukon Territory

Fairbanks

Iditarod Gold Rush Trail   Valdez-Richardson Gold Rush Trail

Marshall **18**   Iditarod **17**   *Susitna River*   Chisana **19**   Canada

Bering Sea   **25**   Matanuska Valley **26**   *Copper River*

McGrath   Willow **30**

Kuskokwim River   Anchorage **24**   Valdez **31**

Cook Inlet **3**   Kennicott

11   Chilkoot Gold Rush Trail

Hope-Sunrise   Katalla **22** **2**   White Pass Gold Rush Trail

Kayak Island   Juneau **8**

Pribilof Islands **5**   *Bristol Bay*   Dalton Gold Rush Trail   British Columbia

Gulf of Alaska

Kiska, Adak & Attu **28** ←   **4**   Sitka **6**

Three Saints Bay

Unalaska **21**

Dutch Harbor **27**   *Pacific Ocean*

Northwest Territories

1902—First oil production, at Katalla (22); telegraph from Eagle to Valdez completed.

1906—Peak gold production year; Alaska granted a nonvoting delegate to Congress.

1911—Copper production begins at Kennicott (23).

1912—Territorial status for Alaska; first Territorial legislature is convened the following year.

1913—First airplane flight in Alaska, at Fairbanks.

1914—Anchorage founded as a work camp for the Alaska Railroad (24).

1916—First bill suggesting Alaska statehood introduced in Congress; peak copper production year.

1922—First pulp mill starts production, Speel River, near Juneau.

1923—President Warren Harding drives spike completing the Alaska Railroad.

1924—Carl Ben Eielson lands at McGrath with the first air mail delivery in Alaska (25).

1935—Matanuska Valley Project begins, which establishes farming families in Alaska (26). First Juneau to Fairbanks flight.

1936—All-time record salmon catch in Alaska—126.4 million fish.

1940—Military buildup in Alaska; Fort Richardson, Elmendorf Air Force Base established. At this point there are only about 40,000 non-Native Alaskans and 32,458 Natives. Pan American Airways inaugurates twice-weekly service between Seattle, Ketchikan and Juneau, using Sikorsky flying boats.

1942—Dutch Harbor bombed (27) and Attu, Adak and Kiska Islands occupied by Japanese forces (28). Alaska Highway built; first overland connection to Lower 48.

1943—Japanese forces driven from Alaska.

1944—Alaska Juneau Mine shuts down.

1953—Oil well drilled near Eureka, on the Glenn Highway, marking the start of modern oil history; first plywood mill at Juneau; first big pulp mill at Ketchikan.

1957—Kenai oil strike.

1958—Statehood measure passed by Congress; statehood proclaimed officially January 3, 1959. Sitka pulp mill opens.

1964—Good Friday earthquake, March 27, causes heavy damage throughout the Gulf Coast region; 131 people lost their lives.

1967—Alaska Centennial celebration; Fairbanks flood.

1968—Oil and gas discoveries at Prudhoe Bay on the North Slope (29); excitement begins. $900 million North Slope oil lease sale the following year; pipeline proposal follows.

1971—Congress approves Alaska Native Land Claims Settlement Act, granting title to 40 million acres of land and providing more than $900 million in payment to Alaska Natives.

1974—Trans-Alaska pipeline receives final approval; construction buildup begins.

1975—Population, labor force soars with construction of pipeline; Alaska Gross Products hits $5.8 billion—double the 1973 figure.

1976—Voters select Willow area (30) for new capital site.

1977—Completion of the trans-Alaska pipeline from Prudhoe Bay to Valdez; shipment of first oil by tanker from Valdez to Puget Sound.

1978—200-mile limit goes into effect; President Jimmy Carter withdraws 56 million acres creating 17 new national monuments as of December 1,1978.

HOLIDAYS

New Year's Day	January 1
Lincoln's Birthday	February 12
Washington's Birthday	Third Monday in February
Seward's Day	Last Monday in March
Memorial Day	Last Monday in May
Independence Day	July 4
Labor Day	First Monday in September
Alaska Day	October 18
Veteran's Day	November 11
Thanksgiving Day	Fourth Thursday in November
Christmas Day	December 25
Sundays and special legal holidays	

Seward's Day commemorates the signing of the treaty by which the United States bought Alaska from Russia, signed on March 30, 1867. Alaska Day is the anniversary of the formal transfer of the territory and the raising of the U.S. flag at Sitka on that date in 1867.

HOTELS AND MOTELS

Although most larger communities offer a choice of accommodations, space may be limited during peak travel times in July and August, so it's wise to make reservations. The Alaska Division of Tourism listed more than 190 hotels and motels in 1979, with low-budget accommodations costing approximately $20 to $30 per night for a double, mid-range hotels, $35 to $45, and first-class hotels, $50 and up. When available, first-class accommodations in rural Alaska can be even more costly. Since rates and addresses change often, contact the Alaska Division of Tourism (Pouch E, Juneau 99811) for up-to-date information.

HUNTING AND SPORT FISHING

Hunting Regulations (1979)

Copies of the complete hunting regulations may be obtained from the Alaska Department of Fish & Game, Subport Building, Juneau 99801, or from any of the many Fish & Game offices throughout the state.

A complete list of registered Alaska guides is available from the Department of Commerce, Division of Occupational Licensing, State of Alaska, Pouch D, Juneau 99811.

Licenses may be obtained from any designated issuing agent or by mail from the Licensing Section, Alaska Department of Revenue, 240 South Franklin, Juneau 99801. They are not available at Department of Fish & Game offices.

Resident license fees: No hunting or trapping license is required of a resident of Alaska under the age of 16, except that all residents, regardless of age, must purchase a $25 tag to hunt brown/grizzly bear. Hunting license, $12; hunting and trapping license, $15; hunting and sport fishing license, $22; hunting, trapping and sport fishing license, $25.

Nonresident regulations: All nonresidents, regardless of age, must have a valid hunting license and tag(s) in their possession while taking or attempting to take game. Metal locking tags may be used to satisfy the tagging requirements for any species for which the tag fee is of equal or less value, but only during the calendar year in which the tag was issued.

Nonresidents are required to have a guide or be accompanied by an Alaskan resident relative over 19 years of age within the second degree of kindred when hunting brown bear, grizzly bear or mountain sheep. Second degree of kindred includes parents, grand-parents, children, grandchildren and sisters or brothers of the person acting as a guide.

Aliens not lawfully admitted to the United States are prohibited from taking game in Alaska or its waters.

Nonresident license fees: Hunting license, $60; hunting and sport fishing license, $90; hunting and trapping license, $200.

Nonresident tag fees: Brown or grizzly bear, $250 each; black bear, $100 each; bison, $250 each; moose, $200 each; sheep, $250 each; caribou, $20 each; elk, goat, $125 each; deer, $35 each; wolf, $50 each; wolverine, $50 each; musk ox, $1,000 each.

Seasons and bag limits: There are 26 game management units in Alaska and wide variety in both seasons and bag limits. In general, seasons for many species of game open around August 1 or September 1.

Marine mammals: Only Eskimos, Indians or Aleuts may hunt marine mammals.

Sport Fishing Regulations (1979)

Resident sport fishing licenses cost $10, valid for the calendar year issued (nonresident, $30; 1-day nonresident, $5; 10-day nonresident, $15). A resident is a person who has maintained a permanent place of abode within the state for 12 consecutive months and has continuously maintained his voting residence in the state; and any member of the military service who has been stationed in the state for the immediately preceding 12 months.

Nearly all sporting goods stores in Alaska sell fishing licenses. They are also available by mail from the Licensing Section, Alaska Department of Revenue, Fish & Game License Division, 240 South Franklin, Juneau 99801.

Alaska Department of Fish & Game has three good publications: *Alaska Sport Fishing Guide; Sport Fishing Predictions;* and *Alaska Sport Fishing Seasons and Bag Limits.* Order from ADF&G, Subport Building, Juneau 99801.

Trophy Fish and Game

RECORD FISH as recorded by the Alaska Department of Fish & Game:

Arctic char/Dolly Varden: 17 pounds, 8 ounces; 36 inches; Wulik River, 1968; Peter Winslow.

Arctic grayling: 4 pounds, 11 ounces; 21½ inches; Ugashik Lake, 1975; Duane Weaver.

Burbot: 24 pounds, 12 ounces; 43 inches; Lake Louise, 1976; George Howard.

Chum salmon: 27 pounds, 3 ounces; 39⅜ inches; Behm Canal, 1977; Robert Jahnke.

Cutthroat trout: 8 pounds, 6 ounces; 26¼ inches; Wilson Lake, 1977; Robert Denison.

Halibut: 440 pounds; 97½ inches; Point Adolphus, 1978; Joar Savland.

King salmon: 91 pounds; 5 inches; Kelp Bay, 1977; Howard Rider.

Kokanee: 2 pounds; 21¼ inches; Lake Lucile, 1977; James E. Gum Jr.

Lake trout: 47 pounds; 44¼ inches; Clarence Lake, 1970; Daniel Thorsness.

Northern pike: 38 pounds; 48 inches; Fish Creek, 15 miles east of Tanana, 1978; Rhoda Edwards.

Pink salmon: 12 pounds, 9 ounces; 30 inches; Moose River, 1974; Stephen Lee.

Rainbow/steelhead: 42 pounds, 2 ounces; 43 inches; Bell Island, 1970; David White.

Red salmon: 16 pounds; 31 inches; Kenai River, 1974; Chuck Leach.

Sheefish: 52 pounds, 8 ounces; 48 inches; Kobuk River, 1968; Jim Keeline.

Silver salmon: 26 pounds; 35 inches; Icy Straits, 1976; Andrew A. Robbin.

Whitefish: 7 pounds, 2 ounces; 25½ inches; Tolovana River, 1978; Glen W. Cornwall.

SPORT FISH SPECIES	BEST BAIT, LURE	MAX. SIZE (LBS.)
Arctic char	spoon, eggs	20
Arctic grayling	flies	5
Brook trout	eggs, spin	5
Burbot	bait	30
Chum salmon	spoon	15
Cutthroat trout	bait, spin, flies	7
Dolly Varden	bait, spin, flies	15
Halibut	octopus, herring	300
King salmon	herring	100
Kokanee	spin, eggs	2
Lake trout	spoon, plug	45
Ling cod	herring	80
Northern pike	spoon, spin	30
Pink salmon	small spoon	10
Rainbow trout	flies, lures, bait	20
Red salmon	flies	15
Rock fish	herring, spin	20
Sheefish	spoon	50
Silver salmon	herring, spoon	25
Steelhead trout	spoon, eggs	45
Whitefish	flies, eggs	10

RECORD BIG GAME as recorded by the Boone and Crockett Club:

Black bear: skull 13 7/16 inches long, 8 6/16 inches wide (1966).

Brown bear (coastal region): skull 17 15/16 inches long, 12 13/16 inches wide (1952).

Grizzly bear (inland): skull 16 10/16 inches long, 9 14/16 inches wide (1970).

Polar bear: skull 18 8/16 inches long, 11 7/16 inches wide (1963).

Bison: right horn 20 4/8 inches long, base circumference 14 7/8 inches; left horn 20 4/8 inches long, base circumference 15 4/8 inches; greatest spread 31 6/8 inches (1965).

Barren Ground caribou: right beam 51 2/8 inches, 22 points; left beam 51 5/8 inches, 23 points (1967).

Mountain goat: right horn 11 5/8 inches long, base circumference 5 6/8 inches; left horn 11 5/8 inches long, base circumference 5 5/8 inches (1933).

Moose: right palm length 46 3/8 inches, width 17 inches; left palm length 51 inches, width 29 6/8 inches; right beam 18 points, left 17 points; greatest spread 77 4/8 inches (taken using an airplane in 1961).

Dall sheep: right horn 48 5/8 inches long, base circumference 14 5/8 inches; left horn 47 7/8 inches long, base circumference 14 6/8 inches (1961).

Musk ox: right horn 26 6/8 inches, left horn 26 4/8 inches, tip-to-tip spread 26 7/8 inches (1976).

ICEBERGS

Icebergs are formed in Alaska wherever glaciers reach salt water or a freshwater lake. Some accessible places in which to view icebergs include Glacier Bay, Icy Bay, Yakutat Bay, Taku Inlet, Endicott Arm, portions of northern Prince William Sound (College Fiord, Barry Arm, Columbia Bay), Mendenhall Lake and Portage Lake.

If icebergs contain little or no sediment, approximately 75% to 80% of their bulk may be underwater. The more sediment an iceberg contains, the greater its density; an iceberg containing large amounts of sediment may even float slightly beneath the surface. Glaciologists of the U.S. Geological Survey believe that some of these "black icebergs" may actually sink to the bottom of a body of water. Since salt water near the faces of glaciers may be liquid to temperatures as low as 28°F, and icebergs melt at 32°F, some of these underwater icebergs may remain unmelted indefinitely.

Alaska's icebergs are comparatively small compared to the icebergs found near Antarctica and Greenland. One of the largest icebergs ever recorded in Alaska was formed in May 1977 in Icy Bay. Glaciologists measured it at 346 feet long, 297 feet wide, and 99 feet above the surface of the water.

ICE, SEA

Sea water generally freezes at minus 2°C or 29°F. Most salt is leached out of sea ice. Ice closest to shore is called shorefast or landfast ice. It attaches itself to shore as freezing begins in fall and slowly builds seaward. Shorefast and other first-year ice may reach thicknesses of up to 6 feet. According to James L. Wise, state climatologist for Arctic Environmental Information Data Center, the mean first-year ice line generally extends farthest south between February and March, following a line that runs approximately from Port Heiden to the Pribilofs, then northwest toward the Siberian coast. During cold winters, it may reach as far south as Cape Sarichef. Chukchi Sea ice generally lasts 6 to 7 months each year; ice covers the Beaufort Sea approximately 9 to 10 months per year, although during some years it may remain year-round.

Permanent pack ice generally occurs north of 72° North latitude. Some pack ice may

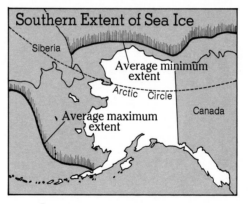

reach thicknesses of 30 feet, though 6 to 12 feet is more common. Currents and winds move pack ice, resulting in leads, or open areas of water. Pressure ridges form between the moving pack ice and shorefast ice. Thicknesses of ice in these ridges may reach 10 to 20 feet above the surface of the water and several times that thickness below the surface.

In 1969 the National Weather Service began a low-profile sea ice reconnaissance program, which expanded greatly during the summer of 1975, when during a year of severe ice, millions of dollars of material had to be shipped to Prudhoe Bay. In 1976, headquarters for a 7-day-a-week ice watch was established at Fairbanks. Personnel base their forecasts on satellite photos and aerial reconnaissance of ice during the height of resupply activities. More recently, rapidly expanding numbers of fishing boats in the Bering Sea have also been using the service.

ICEWORM

Although generally regarded as a hoax, iceworms actually exist. Small, thin, segmented black worms, usually less than one inch long, thrive at temperatures just above freezing. Observers as far back as the 1880's report that at dawn, dusk or on overcast days, the tiny worms, all belonging to the genus *Mesenchytraeus*, may literally carpet the surface of glaciers. When sunlight strikes them, they burrow back down into the ice.

The town of Cordova commemorates its own version of the iceworm each February in the Iceworm Festival, when a 150-foot-long, multi-legged "iceworm" marches in a parade down Main Street.

INFORMATION SOURCES

Agriculture: State Division of Agriculture, Box 800, Palmer 99645; Cooperative Extension Service, University of Alaska, Fairbanks 99701.

Business: Department of Commerce & Economic Development, Division of Economic Enterprise, Pouch EE, Juneau 99811; State Chamber of Commerce, 310 Second Street, Juneau 99801. A 60-page booklet titled *Establishing a Business in Alaska* may be obtained from Economic Enterprize, Pouch EE, Juneau, 99811.

Education: Department of Education, Pouch F, Juneau 99811; U.S. Bureau of Indian Affairs, Box 3-8000, Juneau 99811.

Health: Department of Health and Social Services, Pouch H, Juneau 99811.

Housing: Alaska State Housing Authority, Box 80, Anchorage 99510.

Hunting and Fishing Regulations: Department of Fish & Game, Subport Building, Juneau 99801.

Job Opportunities: State Employment Service, Box 3-7000, Juneau 99811.

Labor: Department of Labor, Box 1149, Juneau 99811.

Land: Division of Lands, 323 East Fourth Avenue, Anchorage 99501; U.S. Bureau of Land Management, 701 C Street, P.O. Box 13, Anchorage 99513.

Mines and Petroleum: State Division of Geological Survey, 3001 Porcupine Drive, Anchorage 99501; Mines Information Office, Pouch M, Juneau 99811; Oil and Gas Conservation Commission, 3001 Porcupine Drive, Anchorage 99501.

Travel and Visitor Information: Division of Tourism, Pouch E, Juneau 99811; Marine Highway Systems, Pouch R, Juneau 99811.

IGLOO

In Alaska, this dwelling is traditionally made of driftwood, whalebone and sod. It is the Canadian Eskimos, not those of Alaska, who built the well-known houses of snow and ice. Alaska Natives, however, did sometimes build temporary shelters and storehouses of snow.

IVORY

Eskimos traditionally carved ivory to make such implements as harpoon heads, dolls and ulu handles. For the past 80 years, however, most carvings have been made to be sold. The bulk of the ivory used today comes from walrus tusks and teeth. Fossil ivory is also used; it may be black, dark brown or beige, depending on the moisture conditions and soil in which it is found. Etching originally was done with hand tools and the scratches were filled in with soot. Today modern power tools supplement the hand tools and carvers color the etching with India ink. The most active carvers live on Saint Lawrence Island, the Seward Peninsula and Little Diomede Island.

JADE

Most Alaskan jade is found near the Dall, Shungnak and Kobuk rivers and Jade Mountain, all north of the Arctic Circle. The stones occur in various shades of green, brown, black, yellow, white and even red. The most valuable are those that are marbled black, white and green. Gem quality jade, about one fourth of the total mined, is used in jewelry making. Fractured jade is used for clock faces, table tops, book ends and other items. Jade is the Alaska state gem.

LANGUAGES

Besides English, Alaska's languages include Haida, Tlingit, Tsimshian, Aleut, several dialects of Eskimo and several dialects of Athabascan.

LODGES, WILDERNESS

Lodges accessible by air or boat can offer samplings of the best of bush Alaska. Amenities vary as greatly as the rates, from simple housekeeping cabins renting for $15 per day to elaborate lodges featuring use of an airplane and/or boat, guided fishing or hunting, and home-cooked meals. Rates for the lodges may vary from $100 to $400 per day per person. In 1979, the Alaska Division of Tourism (Pouch E, Juneau 99811) published addresses of 100 wilderness lodges. The Guide Post® in *ALASKA*® magazine lists addresses for many wilderness lodges.

MOSQUITOES

Twenty-five species of mosquitoes are found in Alaska, the females of all species feeding on people, other mammals or birds. No Alaska mosquitoes carry diseases. The insects are present from April through September in many areas of the state. From Cook Inlet south, they concentrate on coastal flats and forested valleys. In the Aleutian Islands, mosquitoes are absent or present only in small numbers. The most serious mosquito infestations occur in moist areas of fields, bogs and forests of Interior Alaska, from Bristol Bay eastward. Mosquitoes are most active at dusk and dawn; low temperatures and high winds decrease their activity.

NATIONAL FORESTS
PARKS AND MONUMENTS

Numbers in parenthesis refer to map.

National Forests

TONGASS NATIONAL FOREST (2), 16 million acres, located in Southeastern, is the nation's largest national forest.

CHUGACH NATIONAL FOREST (1), 4.7 million acres, comprises areas in Prince William Sound, eastern Kenai Peninsula and Copper River Delta.

Both forests are administered by the U.S. Forest Service, Department of Agriculture.

National Parks and Monuments

Fifty-six million acres of federal land in Alaska were designated national monuments in a presidential proclamation December 1, 1978. The lands were part of 99 million acres set aside earlier by the secretary of the interior for study after Congress failed to pass legislation on Alaska lands during its 1978 session.

The proclamation, under the 1906 Antiquities Act, established 14 new national monuments and enlarged three existing areas, which more than doubled the national park system nationwide.

National parks and monuments are areas of scientific or historic significance. There are three main differences between them. Parks are fairly spacious; monuments may be any size. Parks generally have two or more unique scenic or scientific values; monuments need only one attribute of scientific or prehistoric significance. (Sitka National Historical Park is not spacious, but of great historical significance.) Parks must be established by an act of Congress; monuments may be established by presidential proclamation or by act of Congress.

Those areas administered by the National Park Service (NPS) ban all sport hunting and new mining and logging. Those administered by the U.S. Fish & Wildlife Service (USF&WS) or the U.S. Forest Service (USFS) allow sport hunting.

Yukon-Charley National Monument (17), 1.72 million acres along the Yukon and Charley rivers near the Canadian border. The area includes a large population of peregrine falcons and historic gold rush sites. (NPS)

Gates of the Arctic National Monument (9), 8.22 million acres in the central Brooks Range. Includes the Arrigetch Peaks and the rolling valleys that are prime habitat for caribou and Dall sheep. (NPS)

Noatak National Monument (16), 5.8 million acres in Northwest Alaska. Includes the Noatak River Valley in the western Brooks Range with its spectacular 65-mile canyon and caribou migration route. (NPS)

Kobuk National Monument (13), 1.71 million acres south of the Noatak area. Includes the Kobuk Dunes and the Onion Portage archaeological site and encompasses the northern range of the Western Arctic caribou herd. (NPS)

Cape Krusenstern National Monument (7), 560,000 acres on the Chukchi Sea near Kotzebue. A series of 114 lateral layers contains artifacts of Eskimo communities dating back 4,000 years and may hold keys to the Bering land bridge. (NPS)

Bering Land Bridge National Monument (6), 2.6 million acres on the north shore of the Seward Peninsula. Contains what is believed to be the last remnants of the Bering land bridge and lies only 50 miles from Russia. (NPS)

Denali National Monument (8), a 3.89-million-acre addition to Mount McKinley National Park. The addition picks up the traditional Indian name for the mountain. (NPS)

Wrangell-Saint Elias National Monument (19), 10.95 million acres in Southcentral and Southeastern Alaska near the Canadian border. The Wrangell and Saint Elias Mountains are the largest collection of peaks above 16,000 feet in the nation. The area is one of the largest unexplored, virtually unmapped areas on the continent. (NPS)

Kenai Fjords National Monument (12), 570,000 acres on the eastern shore of the Kenai Peninsula. The area includes the Harding Icefield and a system of fjords along most of the eastern Kenai coastline. Since the area is not traditional subsistence hunting grounds, any hunting is banned from the area. (NPS)

Lake Clark National Monument (14), 2.5 million acres inland from the western shore of Cook Inlet. The monument includes Lake Clark, the Chigmit Mountains and two active volcanoes. (NPS)

Katmai National Monument (11), a 1.37-million-acre addition to an existing monument transecting the Alaska Peninsula. (NPS)

Aniakchak National Monument (4), 350,000 acres on the Alaska Peninsula. The main feature is the Aniakchak caldera, a 30-square-mile crater which holds lava flows and explosion pits. (NPS)

Glacier Bay National Monument (10), a 550,000-acre addition to an existing monument 100 miles west of Juneau. (NPS)

Becharof Lake National Monument (5), 1.2 million acres on the Alaska Peninsula. The area includes Becharof Lake and Mount Peulik, an active volcano, whose system includes some of the few known volcanic mars in the world. (USF&WS)

Yukon Flats National Monument (18), 10.6 million acres along the Yukon River between Stevens Village and Circle. The area includes some of the most important waterfowl nesting areas in the state. (USF&WS)

Admiralty Island National Monument (3), 1.1 million acres, which includes the bulk of the island. Sport hunting, fishing, camping and valid mining claims will continue. (USFS)

Misty Fjords National Monument (15), 2.2 million acres along the mainland and Revillagigedo Island shorelines of Southeastern Alaska. Highlights of the area along the Behm Canal include Walker Cove and Rudyerd Bay. (USFS)

INFORMATION:

The National Park Service, 540 West Fifth Avenue, Anchorage 99501. (A permanent display of photographs from areas throughout the state may be seen at the same address. Films of various Alaskan subjects are shown daily, Monday through Friday, at 12:15 P.M. all year. Films and slide shows of national parks and monuments in Alaska are shown at 2:30 P.M. during the summer months only. There is no charge. The information office telephone number is 271-4243.)

U.S. Forest Service, P.O. Box 1628, Juneau 99802.

U.S. Fish & Wildlife Service, 1011 East Tudor Road, Anchorage 99504.

Glacier Bay National Monument (10)	2,803,840 acres*
P.O. Box 1089, Juneau 99802	established 1925
Katmai National Monument (11)	2,792,137 acres†
P.O. Box 7, King Salmon 99613	established 1918
Klondike Gold Rush National Historical Park (20)	13,300 acres
P.O. Box 517, Skagway 99840	established 1977
Mount McKinley National Park (21)	1,939,493 acres††
P.O. Box 9, McKinley Park 99755	established 1917
Sitka National Historical Park (22)	54 acres
P.O. Box 738, Sitka 99835	established 1910

*3,353,840 acres as of December 1, 1978
†4,162,137 acres as of December 1, 1978
††5,829,493 acres as of December 1, 1978, with addition of Denali National Monument

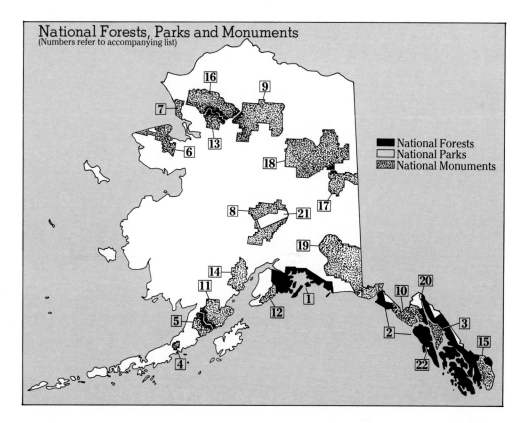

National Forests, Parks and Monuments
(Numbers refer to accompanying list)

National Forests
National Parks
National Monuments

NATIONAL HISTORIC PLACES

The National Register of Historic Places includes national, state and local sites worthy of preservation. Properties may be nominated by states or by federal agencies and are placed on the register by approval of the secretary of the interior. The list includes Alaska's Sitka National Historical Park and Klondike Gold Rush National Historical Park. Historic sites and structures of national significance are eligible for designation as National Historic Landmarks; these are shown with an asterisk (*) in the list below. Those marked (**) are eligible for the register but not entered as of July 1979.

Southeastern

Alaska Native Brotherhood Hall	Sitka
Alaska Steam Laundry	Juneau
Alaska Totems	Ketchikan
Alaskan Hotel	Juneau
American Flag Raising Site*	Sitka
Bergmann Hotel	Juneau
Bering Expedition Landing	Kayak Island
Cable House and Station	Sitka
Cape Spencer Lighthouse	Cape Spencer
Chief Shakes House	Wrangell
Chilkoot Trail, Mile 0 to Canadian Border*	Chilkoot Pass Area
Crab Bay Petroglyph**	Crab Bay
Eldred Rock Lighthouse	Lynn Canal
Emmons House	Sitka
Father William Duncan Cottage	Metlakatla
Fort Durham, Taku Harbor	Juneau vicinity
Fort William H. Seward	Haines
Government School	Sitka
Governor's Mansion	Juneau
Hidden Falls Site**	Sitka vicinity
Holy Trinity Church	Juneau
Klondike Gold Rush National Historical Park*	Skagway area
Mills, May House	Sitka
Mills, W.P. House	Sitka
New Russia Archaeological Site	Yakutat
Pleasant Camp	Haines Highway
Redoubt St. Archangel Michael Site, Old Sitka*	Sitka vicinity
Russian Mission Orphanage*	Sitka
St. Michael's Cathedral*	Sitka
St. Nicholas Church (Russian Orthodox)	Juneau
St. Peter's Church	Sitka
See House	Sitka
Sheldon Jackson Museum	Sitka
Sitka National Historical Park	Sitka
Skagway and White Pass District*	Taiya Inlet, Lynn Canal
Totem Bight	Ketchikan
U.S. Army Corps of Engineers, Storehouse #3	Portland Canal
U.S. Army Corps of Engineers, Storehouse #4	Hyder
Wickersham, House of	Juneau
Wrangell Public School	Wrangell

Southcentral

AHRS Site KOD-207, Long Island	Kodiak area
Alaska Nellie's Homestead	Lawing vicinity
Anderson (Oscar) House	Anchorage
Assumption of the Virgin Mary, Church of*	Kenai
Ballaine House	Seward
Beluga Point Archaeological Site	North Shore, Turnagain Arm
Bering Expedition Landing*	Kayak Island
Campus Center Archaeological Site	Anchorage
Chilkat Oil Refinery Site	Katalla
Chitina Tin Shop	Chitina
Chugach Island Archaeological Site	Kachemak Bay
Coal Village	Kachemak Bay
Cooper Landing Post Office	Cooper Landing
Copper River and Northwestern Railway	Chitina vicinity
Cordova Post Office	Cordova
Crow Creek Mine	Girdwood
Cunningham-Hall PT-6 NC692W (aircraft)	Palmer
Dakah De'nin's Village Site	Chitina
Diversion Tunnel, Lowell Creek	Seward
Erskine House*	Kodiak
Federal Building (Old)	Anchorage
Fort Abercrombie	Kodiak
Hirshey Mine	Hope vicinity
Holy Resurrection, Church of the	Kodiak
Holy Transfiguration of Our Lord Chapel	Ninilchik
Hope Historic District	Hope vicinity
Independence Mines	Hatcher Pass
Kaguyak Village Site	Kodiak Island
Knik Site	Knik vicinity
Moose River Site, Naptowne	Kenai area
Nabesna Gold Mine	Nabesna area
Palmer Depot	Palmer
Palugvik Site*	Hawkins Island
Rebarchek (Raymond), Colony Farm	Palmer area

Southcentral (continued)

St. Nicholas Church (Russian Orthodox)	Eklutna
Selenie Lagoon Archaeological Site	Port Graham vicinity
Susitna River Bridge, Alaska Railroad	Talkeetna vicinity
Swetman House	Seward
Teeland's General Store	Wasilla
Three Saints Site*	Kodiak Island
Tunnel #1, Alaska Central Railroad	Seward vicinity
Wasilla Depot	Wasilla
Yukon Island, Main Site*	Yukon Island

Western

Ananiulak Island Archaeological District*	Aleutian Islands
Archaeological Site 49 Af3	Katmai National Monument
Archaeological Site 49 Mk10	Katmai National Monument
Brooks River Archaeological District	Katmai National Monument
Cape Krusenstern Archaeological District*	Kotzebue vicinity
Cape Nome Mining District Discovery Sites*	Nome
Cape Nome Roadhouse	Nome vicinity
Carrighar (Sally) House	Nome
Chaluka Site*	Umnak Island
Chugachik Island Archaeological Site	Homer vicinity
Donaldson, Lieutenant C.V.	Nome
Fort St. Michael Site	Nome vicinity
Fur Seal Rookeries*	Pribilof Islands
Gambell Sites*	St. Lawrence Island
Holy Ascension, Church of	Unalaska
Iyatayet Archaeological Site*	Norton Sound
Kijik Historic District	Lake Clark vicinity
Kukak Village Site 49 Mk6	Katmai National Monument
McClain (Carrie) House	Nome
Norge Landing Site	Teller
Onion Portage Archaeological Site*	Kiana vicinity
Pilgrim Hot Springs	Seward Peninsula
Port Moller Hot Springs Village Site	Alaska Peninsula
Redoubt St. Michael Site	Nome vicinity
Savonski River Archaeological District	Naknek vicinity
Sitka Spruce Plantation*	Amaknak Island
Takli Island Archaeological District	Katmai National Monument
Wales Complex*	Wales vicinity

Interior

Archaeological Site KAR-037**	Karluk
Central House	Central
Creamer's Dairy	Fairbanks
Cripple Creek Site**	Steese Highway
Davidson Ditch**	Steese Highway
Dry Creek Site*	Healy vicinity
Eagle Historic District*	Eagle
Federal Building, U.S. Post Office, Courthouse	Fairbanks
Gakona Roadhouse	Gakona
Harding Car, Alaskaland	Fairbanks vicinity
Immaculate Conception Church	Fairbanks
Kennecott Mines	McCarthy vicinity
The Kink	Forty Mile River
Kolmakov Redoubt Site, Kuskokwim River	Aniak vicinity
McCarthy General Store	McCarthy
McCarthy Power Plant	McCarthy
Mission Church	Arctic Village
Mission House (Old)	Fort Yukon
Nenana Depot	Nenana
Porcupine Historic District	Northeast Alaska
Rainey's Cabin	Fairbanks
Rika's Landing	Delta
Sourdough Lodge*	Gulkana vicinity
Sternwheeler Nenana	Fairbanks
Tanana Mission	Tanana
Tangle Lakes Archaeological District	Paxson vicinity
Teklanika Archaeological District	Mount McKinley National Park
Thomas (George C.) Library*	Fairbanks
U.S. Bureau of Mines Safety Car #5	Suntrana
Wickersham House	Fairbanks

Far North

Birnirk Site*	Barrow
Gallagher Flint Station Archaeological Site	Sagwon
Ipiutak Archaeological Site*	Point Hope
Leffingwell Camp*	Flaxman Island

NATIONAL WILDLIFE
REFUGES AND RANGES

In the Lower 48, ranges are those areas withdrawn from public domain, primarily for the protection of game species; refuges were acquired in fee through outright purchase. In Alaska, all these lands were withdrawn from public domain, and the two terms are used interchangeably; there are few differences between a range and a refuge. Both are important in preserving wildlife resources; providing nesting, feeding and resting areas for migratory birds; protecting endangered wildlife; and preserving ecologically important associations of animal and plant life. The first Alaskan wildlife refuges were established during the period 1909 to 1912. Two, Becharof Lake and Yukon Flats, were declared as national monuments in December of 1978. In addition, some 40 million acres were withdrawn for 20 years by the Secretary of the Interior in February of 1980, after Congress failed to act on pending Alaska lands legislation. (These lands are not listed here or reflected on the accompanying map.) Final congressional action on an Alaska lands bill could modify or nullify the withdrawals made by the Secretary of the Interior at that time.

Some acreage figures on the accompanying list include submerged lands (marine habitat).

Information: Area Supervisor, Alaska Wildlife Refuges, U.S. Fish & Wildlife Service, 1011 East Tudor Road, Anchorage 99504.

NAME AND MAJOR FEATURES	ADMINISTRATIVE ADDRESS
1. Aleutian Islands National Wildlife Refuge (1913), 2,720,225 acres. Sea birds; sea otters.	Box 5251 Adak 98791
2. William O. Douglas Arctic Wildlife Range (1960), (Formerly Arctic National Wildlife Range) 8,894,624 acres. Undisturbed arctic ecosystem.	Room 266, Federal Building and Courthouse 101 12th Avenue, Box 20 Fairbanks 99701
3. Becharof National Monument (national monument declared 1978; administered by U.S. Fish & Wildlife Service) 1,200,000 acres. Dense brown bear population.	1011 East Tudor Road Anchorage 99503
4. Bering Sea National Wildlife Refuge (1909), 85,197 acres. Nesting sea birds; one of the largest fulmar colonies in existence.	Box 346 Bethel 99559
5. Bogoslof National Wildlife Refuge (1909), 335 acres. Sea bird rookeries; large murre and sea lion colonies.	Box 5251 Adak 98791
6. Cape Newenham National Wildlife Refuge (1969), 265,000 acres. Possibly largest sea bird nesting area in North America.	Box 346 Bethel 99559
7. Chamisso National Wildlife Refuge (1912), 426 acres. Important arctic sea bird nesting area.	Box 346 Bethel 99559
8. Clarence Rhode National Wildlife Range (1960), 2,887,026 acres. Migratory bird nesting area; especially cackling Canada geese, black brant, emperor geese.	Box 346 Bethel 99559
9. Forrester Island National Wildlife Refuge (1912), 2,832 acres. Cliff-nesting sea birds—murres, puffins, auklets, gulls.	Area Supervisor, Alaska Wildlife Refuges, 1011 East Tudor Road, Anchorage 99503
10. Hazen Bay National Wildlife Refuge (1937), 6,800 acres. Similar to Clarence Rhode NWR.	Box 346 Bethel 99559
11. Hazy Islands National Wildlife Refuge (1912), 30 acres. Sea bird colonies.	Area Supervisor, Alaska Wildlife Refuges, 1011 East Tudor Road, Anchorage 99503
12. Izembek National Wildlife Range (1960), 320,801 acres. Continent's entire brant population feeds here; many other species of waterfowl.	Pouch 2 Cold Bay 99571
13. Kenai National Moose Range (1941), 1,730,000 acres. Moose management; other big game; trumpeter swan; other waterfowl.	Box 500 Kenai 99611
14. Kodiak National Wildlife Refuge (1941), 1,815,000 acres. Brown bear; major salmon runs.	Box 825 Kodiak 99615

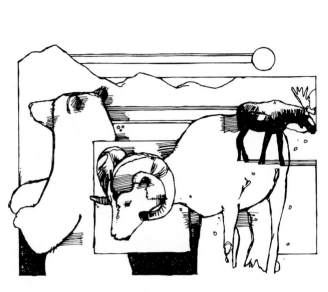

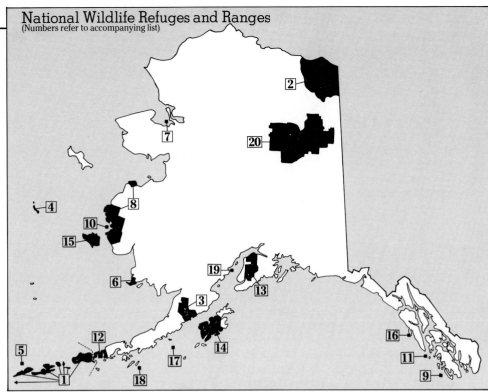

National Wildlife Refuges and Ranges
(Numbers refer to accompanying list)

NAME AND MAJOR FEATURES	ADMINISTRATIVE ADDRESS
15. Nunivak National Wildlife Refuge (1929), 3,330,630 acres. Musk ox; reindeer; brant; Canada geese; sea birds.	Box 346 Bethel 99559
16. Saint Lazaria National Wildlife Refuge (1909), 65 acres. Seabird rookeries.	Area Supervisor, Alaska Wildlife Refuges, 1011 East Tudor Road, Anchorage 99503
17. Semidi National Wildlife Refuge (1932), 251,930 acres. Sea lions; fulmars, puffins, auklets, petrels, murres, kittiwakes.	Pouch 2 Cold Bay 99571
18. Simeonof National Wildlife Refuge (1958), 25,855 acres. Sea otter.	Pouch 2 Cold Bay 99571
19. Tuxedni National Wildlife Refuge (1909), 5,411 acres. Vast black-legged kittiwake colony; sea birds.	Box 500 Kenai, 99611
20. Yukon Flats National Monument (national monument declared 1978; administered by U.S. Fish & Wildlife Service) 10,600,000 acres. Waterfowl nesting area.	1011 East Tudor Road Anchorage 99503

In addition, Saint Matthew, Saint Lawrence and the Pribilof Islands have specialized refuges.
(See also *National Forests, Parks and Monuments; National Historic Places; State Park System.*)

181

NATIVES

Of the total population of Alaska Natives, roughly 40,000 are Eskimos, 25,000 are Indians and 7,000 are Aleuts. Many live in widely separated villages along the coastline and great rivers of the state. The village, rather than the tribe, is the unit; the Alaska tribe is the language group. Natives are migrating to the cities; about 5,000 live in Fairbanks, 10,000 in Anchorage.

At the time of European discovery in 1741, the Eskimo, Indian and Aleut people lived within well-defined regions, and there was little mixing of ethnic groups. In Southeastern, the salmon, deer and other plentiful foods permitted the Tlingit, Tsimshian and Haida Indians to settle in permanent villages and develop a culture rich in art. The Athabascan Indians of the Interior followed the migrating caribou and took advantage of seasonal abundance of fish, waterfowl and other game. The Eskimos and Aleuts, like the Tlingits, depended on the sea, but developed a way of life suited to a hostile climate.

The Tsimshians migrated in 1887 from their former home in British Columbia to Annette Island, under Anglican minister Father William Duncan. About 1,000 now live in Metlakatla and cooperatively run a salmon cannery, four fish traps, a water system, a hydroelectric plant and a logging industry. Like all Southeastern people, they are primarily fishermen.

Between 700 and 800 Haidas live in Alaska, about 200 of whom live in Hydaburg on the south end of Prince of Wales Island. They immigrated from Canada in the 1700's. More than 1,100 live in Canada's Queen Charlotte Islands. Haidas excelled in the art of totem carving and are noted for fine slate carvings and precise and delicate working of wood, bone and shell.

About 10,000 to 12,000 Tlingits are well distributed in Southeastern; another 1,000 live in other areas of the state, primarily in the Anchorage area. Tlingits, who arrived from Canada before the first European contact, commercially dominated the Interior Canadian Indians, trading eulachon oil, copper pieces and Chilkat blankets for various furs. Like the Haidas, they are part of the totem culture that has attracted so much attention in Southeastern. The totems provided a historic record of major events in the life of a family or clan.

The Athabascans, before European contact, were nomadic. There was no agriculture. They are closely related to the Navajos and Apaches of Southwestern United States. The approximately 7,000 Athabascans all speak similar languages.

The Aleuts have traditionally lived on the Alaska Peninsula, eastward to the Ugashik River on the north and to Pavlof Bay on the south, extending down the Aleutian Chain and nearby islands. When the Russians reached the Aleutians in the 1740's, there were an estimated 16,000 to 20,000 Aleuts and practically every island was inhabited, but now only a few have permanent Aleut settlements. Some live on the Pribilof Islands, where they work for the U.S. government in handling the seal herds.

The Aleuts lived in permanent villages, taking advantage of sea life and land mammals for food. The original houses were large, communal structures, partly buried; later houses were small, single-family units. Today they live in frame houses, and many are commercial fishermen. Their language is related to the Eskimo, but far removed. The Aleuts are

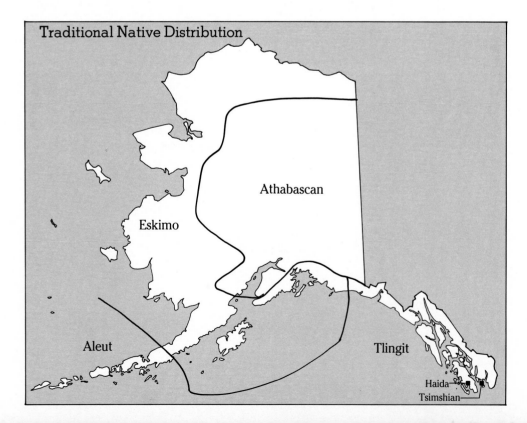

Traditional Native Distribution

Athabascan

Eskimo

Aleut

Tlingit

Haida
Tsimshian

divided into two groups speaking slightly different dialects.

The Eskimos have traditionally lived in villages along the harsh Bering Sea and Arctic Ocean coastlines, and extended southward along the Gulf of Alaska coast. They took salmon, waterfowl, berries, ptarmigan and a few caribou, but it was in sea and ice hunting that they excelled. Whales, seals and walrus were the mainstay of their economy. Houses were partly buried and covered with sod; they did not build snow igloos.

Alaska Native Regional Corporations

Regional corporations were formed under the Alaska Native Land Claims Settlement Act to administer the cash receipts of more than $900 million and land selections of 40 million acres. The act was passed in 1971 as compensation for loss of lands historically occupied by the Natives of Alaska. The regional corporations are business corporations designed to manage these assets. A 13th corporation, for those Natives who reside outside Alaska, has been organized.

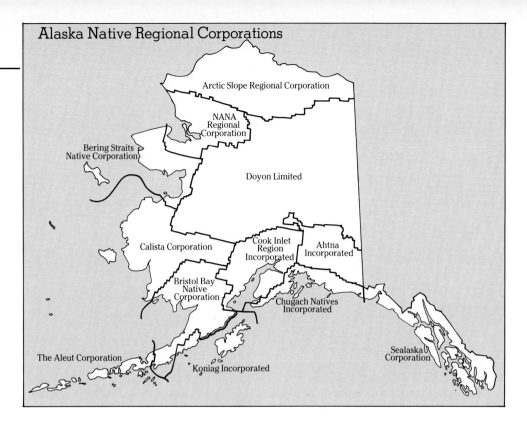

Alaska Native Regional Corporations

Ahtna Incorporated
P.O. Box 823
Copper Center 99573
or
515 D Street, Room 202
Anchorage 99501   Copper River Basin

Aleut Corporation
833 Gambell Street
Anchorage 99501   Aleutian Islands

Arctic Slope Regional
Corporation
P.O. Box 129
Barrow 99723   Arctic Alaska

Bering Straits Native
Corporation
P.O. Box 1008
Nome 99762   Seward Peninsula

Bristol Bay Native
Corporation
P.O. Box 198
Dillingham 99576
or
445 Fifth Avenue
Anchorage 99501   Bristol Bay Area

Calista Corporation
516 Denali Street
Anchorage 99501
or
P.O. Box 408   Yukon-Kuskokwim
Bethel 99559   Delta

Chugach Natives, Inc.
912 East 15th Avenue   Prince William
Anchorage 99501   Sound

Cook Inlet Region, Inc.
2525 C Street
P.O. Drawer 4-N
Anchorage 99509   Cook Inlet Region

Doyon Limited
First and Hall Streets
Fairbanks 99701   Interior Alaska

Koniag, Inc.
P.O. Box 746
Kodiak 99615   Kodiak Area

NANA Regional Corporation, Inc.
P.O. Box 49
Kotzebue 99752   Kobuk Region

Sealaska Corporation
One Sealaska Plaza, Suite 400
Juneau 99801   Southeastern Alaska

The 13th Regional Corporation
1800 Westlake Avenue N, Suite 313
Seattle 98109

PERMAFROST

Permanently frozen subsoil, continuous in polar regions, underlies the entire arctic region to depths reported to reach 2,000 feet. Permafrost influences construction in the Arctic because building on it causes thawing and therefore heaving of the melted ground.

Much of the Interior and some of Southcentral are also underlain by permafrost. It is responsible for thousands of lakes dotting the arctic tundra because ground water is held on the surface.

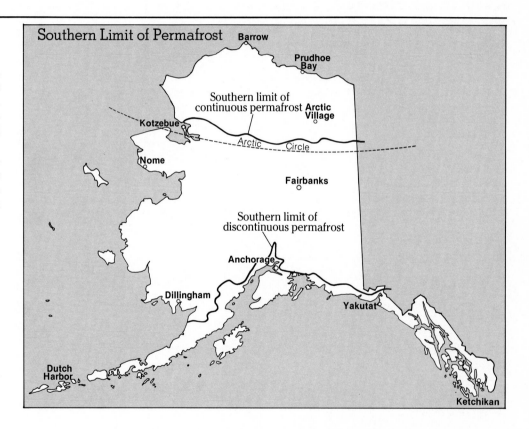

Southern Limit of Permafrost

STATE PARK SYSTEM

Alaska has five state parks: Chugach State Park, Denali State Park, Chilkat State Park, Kachemak Bay State Park and Wood-Tikchik State Park. In addition, the agency administers a system of 50 highway waysides, 5 recreation areas, 4 historic sites, 2 trail systems and 1 wilderness park. Some of the facilities listed below also offer trails and boat launching ramps. All facilities are available on a first-come, first-served basis. General information on the state park system is available by contacting the Division of Parks, 619 Warehouse Avenue, Suite 210, Anchorage 99501. Numbers on the opposite list refer to the map on page 186.

	ACREAGE	CAMPING UNITS	PICNIC UNITS	NEAREST TOWN
SOUTHEAST DISTRICT (Box 142, Sitka 99835)				
Mosquito Lake Wayside (1)	5	13		Haines
Chilkoot Trail (2)	635			Skagway
Chilkoot Lake Wayside (3)	80	32		Haines
Liarsville Wayside (4)	2	7		Skagway
Portage Cove Wayside (5)	7	9		Haines
Juneau Trail System (6)				Juneau
Old Sitka Historic Site (7)	51			Sitka
Halibut Point Wayside (8)	22		9	Sitka
Baranof Castle Hill Historic Site (9)	1			Sitka
Pat's Lake Campground (10)	198	9		Wrangell
Totem Bight Historic Site (11)	10			Ketchikan
Refuge Cove Picnic Wayside (12)	13		14	Ketchikan
Chilkat State Park (13)	6,045			Haines
INTERIOR DISTRICT (4420 Airport Way, Fairbanks 99701)				
Gardiner Creek Wayside (14)	20			Tok
Deadman Lake Wayside (15)	20			Tok
Lakeview Wayside (16)	440	8		Tok
Tok River Wayside (17)	8	10		Tok
Moon Lake Wayside (18)	114	15		Tok
Clearwater Wayside (19)	29	12		Delta Junction
Harding Lake Recreation Area (20)	95	89	52	North Pole
Salcha River Picnic Wayside (21)	59		20	North Pole
Chena River Wayside (22)	27		101	Fairbanks
Chena River Recreation Area (23)	254,080			Fairbanks
Chatanika River Wayside (24)	73	25		Fairbanks
Donnelly Creek Wayside (25)	20	12		Delta Junction
Eagle Trail Wayside (26)	640	40	4	Tok
Quartz Lake Wayside (27)	280			Delta Junction

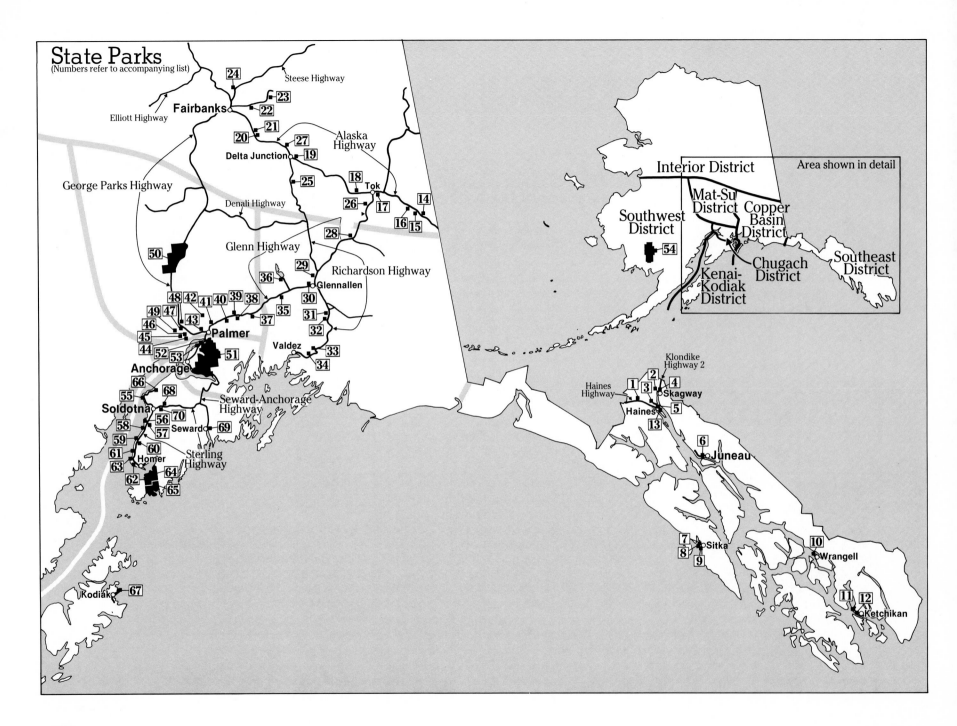

State Parks
(Numbers refer to accompanying list)

	ACREAGE	CAMPING UNITS	PICNIC UNITS	NEAREST TOWN
MAT-SU DISTRICT (P.O. Box 182, Palmer 99645)				
Matanuska Glacier Wayside (37)	231	6		Palmer
Long Lake Wayside (38)	372	8		Palmer
Bonnie Lake Wayside (39)	31	8		Palmer
King Mountain Wayside (40)	20	22		Palmer
Moose Creek Wayside (41)	40	8		Palmer
Independence Mine State Historical Park (42)	271			Palmer
Finger Lake Wayside (43)	47	41		Palmer
Big Lake (South) Wayside (44)	16	13	6	Wasilla
Big Lake (East) Wayside (45)	19	15		Wasilla
Rocky Lake Wayside (46)	48	10		Wasilla
Lake Nancy Wayside (47)	35	30	30	Willow
Willow Creek Wayside (48)	90	17		Willow
Lake Nancy Recreation Area (49)	22,685			Willow
South Rolly Lake Campground		106	20	Willow
Denali State Park (50)	336,480			Cantwell
Byers Lake Campground		61		Cantwell
COPPER BASIN DISTRICT (P.O. Box 182, Palmer 99645)				
Porcupine Creek Wayside (28)	240	12		Tok
Dry Creek Wayside (29)	128	58	4	Glennallen
Tolsona Creek Wayside (30)	600	5		Glennallen
Squirrel Creek Wayside (31)	325	7		Copper Center
Little Tonsina Wayside (32)	102	6		Copper Center
Worthington Glacier Wayside (33)	113	6		Valdez
Blueberry Lake Wayside (34)	192	6		Valdez
Little Nelchina Wayside (35)	22	6		Glennallen
Lake Louise Wayside (36)	50	6		Glennallen

	ACREAGE	CAMPING UNITS	PICNIC UNITS	NEAREST TOWN
CHUGACH DISTRICT (2601 Commercial Drive, Anchorage 99501)				
Chugach State Park (51)	495,204			Anchorage
Eklutna Basin Campgrounds		30		Eagle River
Thunder Bird Falls			6	Eagle River
Eagle River		36	12	Eagle River
Upper Huffman Picnic Area	58			Anchorage
McHugh Creek			30	Anchorage
Bird Creek		25	14	Anchorage
Mirror Lake Wayside (52)	90		30	Eagle River
Peters Creek Wayside (53)	52	32		Eagle River
SOUTHWEST DISTRICT (619 Warehouse Ave., Suite 210, Anchorage 99501)				
Wood-Tikchik State Park (54)	1,428,329			Dillingham
KENAI-KODIAK DISTRICT (Box 1247, Soldotna 99669)				
Bernice Lake Wayside (55)	7	11		Kenai
Kasilof River Wayside (56)	47	11		Soldotna
Johnson Lake Wayside (57)	56	20		Soldotna
Clam Gulch Picnic Wayside (58)			20	Soldotna
Ninilchik Wayside (59)	15	15		Ninilchik
Deep Creek Wayside (60)	44		10	Ninilchik
Stariski Creek Wayside (61)	30	12		Anchor Point
Silver King Wayside (62)	174	38		Anchor Point
Anchor River Wayside (63)	57	7		Anchor Point
Kachemak Bay State Park (64)	119,970	5		Seldovia
Kachemak Bay Wilderness Park (65)	208,320			Seldovia
Captain Cook Recreation Area (66)	3,620			Kenai
Discovery Campground		57		Kenai
Discovery Picnic Area			28	Kenai
Swanson River Canoe Landing				Kenai
Stormy Lake		10	40	Kenai
Bishop Creek		12		Kenai
Fort Abercrombie (67)	183	14		Kodiak
Izaak Walton Wayside (68)	8	32		Soldotna
Caines Head Recreation Area (69)	5,961			Seward
Funny River Wayside (70)	14			Soldotna

TIDES

In Southeast Alaska, Prince William Sound, Cook Inlet and Bristol Bay, salt water undergoes extreme daily fluctuations, creating powerful tidal currents. Some bays may go totally dry at low tide. The second greatest tide range in North America occurs in Upper Cook Inlet where, near Anchorage, the maximum diurnal range during spring tides is 38.9 feet. Here are diurnal ranges for some coastal communities:

	FEET
Bethel	4.0
Cold Bay	7.1
Cordova	12.4
Haines	16.8
Herschel Island	0.7
Ketchikan	15.4
Kodiak	8.5
Naknek River entrance	22.6
Nikiski	20.7
Nome	1.6
Nushagak	19.6
Point Barrow	0.4
Port Heiden	12.3
Port Moller	10.8
Sand Point	7.3
Sitka	9.9
Valdez	12.0
Whittier	12.3
Wrangell	15.7
Yakutat	10.1

TIME ZONES

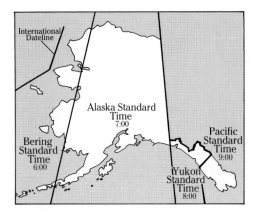

TOTEMS

Totems, carved from yellow cedar, are a traditional art form among the Indians of British Columbia and Southeastern Alaska. Although most well-known totems are tall and free-standing, totemic art also was applied to houseposts and short entrance poles. The carved monuments were erected by the leading clans in each tribe in memory of their chiefs who had died. The poles also symbolized power and prestige.

The figures carved on totem poles were the crests of their owners and varied with each family and clan. Selection of crests to be used on the poles was left to the fancy of the owners. Few rules governed the order of figures along the carved shaft, although the most important crest generally was on top.

Animals of the region are most often represented on the poles. Of all the crests, the frog appears most frequently, then the bear, eagle, raven, thunderbird, wolf, owl, grouse, starfish, finback whale and halibut. Also represented are figures from Indian mythology: monsters with animal features, human-like spirits and semi-historical ancestors. Occasionally depicted are objects, devices, masks and charms, and most rarely, art illustrating plants and sky phenomena.

The poles are traditionally painted with pigments made from coal, earth of yellow, brown and red hues, cinnabar, berry juice and spruce sap. Fungus found on hemlock produces various colors: yellow when decayed, red when roasted, and black when charred. Before modern paints became available, salmon eggs chewed with cedar bark formed the case, or glue, for the paint.

Totem art reached its peak after 1830, with the introduction of steel European tools acquired through fur trade. Leading families competed with others, building larger and more elaborate totem poles to show their wealth and prestige.

The pole was left to stand as long as nature unaided would permit, usually no more than 50 to 60 years. Once a pole became so rotten that it fell, it was pushed aside, left to decay naturally or used for firewood. Most totem poles still standing in parks today are 40 to 50 years old. Heavy precipitation and acid muskeg soils hasten decomposition.

Easily accessible collections of totem poles may be seen in Ketchikan, Wrangell and Sitka. Carvers may be seen practicing their art in Haines and Sitka.

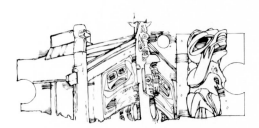

TRANS-ALASKA PIPELINE

The pipeline designer, builder and operator is the Alyeska Pipeline Service Company, a consortium of the following eight oil companies:

Sohio Pipe Line Company	33.34%
ARCO Pipe Line Company	21.00%
Exxon Pipeline Company	20.00%
BP Pipelines Inc.	15.84%
Mobil Alaska Pipeline Company	5.00%
Union Alaska Pipeline Company	1.66%
Phillips Petroleum Company	1.66%
Amerada Hess Pipeline Corporation	1.50%

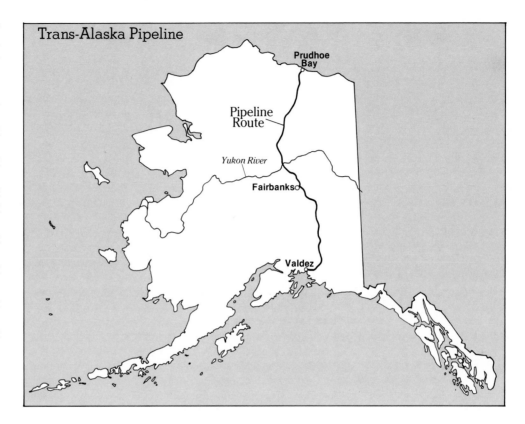

Trans-Alaska Pipeline

Pipeline length: 800 miles, slightly less than half that length buried, the remainder on 78,000 above-ground supports.

Pipe size: 48 inches in diameter, before construction in lengths of 40 feet; thickness varies from 0.462 inch to 0.562 inch.

Pipeline capacity: 1.16 million barrels a day initially; can be increased with additional pumping stations and terminal facilities to 2 million barrels a day.

Estimated crude oil reserves recoverable on the North Slope: 9.4 billion barrels. Estimated hydrocarbon reserves: 26.5 trillion cubic feet.

Valdez ship-loading capacity: 110,000 barrels per hour for each of 3 berths; 80,000 barrels per hour for 1 berth.

Length of pipeline haul road: 360 miles, from the Yukon River to Prudhoe Bay, including the first bridge (2,290 feet long) spanning the Yukon in Alaska.

Important dates: Haul road construction began April 29, 1974, and was completed 154 days later. First pipe was installed, in the Tonsina River, March 27, 1975. First oil left Prudhoe Bay June 20, 1977, and reached the Valdez Terminal July 28. First tanker load of oil was shipped August 1, 1977, aboard the S.S. *ARCO Juneau.* Tanker number 1,000, the S.S. *ARCO Heritage,* sailed June 13, 1979.

UNIVERSITIES
AND COLLEGES

ALASKA PACIFIC UNIVERSITY
University Drive, Anchorage 99504

INUPIAT UNIVERSITY OF THE ARCTIC
Barrow 99723
The focus of this institution is preservation of the Inupiat Eskimo culture. There is no tuition charge for residents of the North Slope Borough; other students may be enrolled by special arrangement.

SHELDON JACKSON COLLEGE
Lincoln and Jeff Davis Streets, Sitka 99835
Autonomous 2-year college affiliated with the United Presbyterian Church. Offers fishery and wildlife management, secretarial science, business administration, logging management, data processing, flight training, forestry, education.

UNIVERSITY OF ALASKA
A state system of 2-year and 4-year institutions, with a variety of academic programs, includes the following schools:

Information
Director of Admissions and Registrar
University of Alaska Statewide System
Fairbanks 99701

Southcentral Region
Anchorage Community College
2533 Providence Drive, Anchorage 99504
University of Alaska, Anchorage
2651 Providence Drive, Anchorage 99504
Kenai Peninsula Community College
Box 657, Kenai 99611
Kodiak Community College
Box 954, Kodiak 99615
Kuskokwim Community College
P.O. Box 368, Bethel 99559
Matanuska-Susitna Community College
Box 86, Palmer 99645
Prince William Sound Community College
P.O. Box 590, Valdez 99686

Southeastern Region
University of Alaska, Juneau
Box 1447, Juneau 99801
Juneau-Douglas Community College
Box 135, Auke Bay 99821
Ketchikan Community College
Box 358, Ketchikan 99901
Sitka Community College
Box 1090, Sitka 99835

Northern Region
University of Alaska, Fairbanks
Fairbanks 99701
Tanana Valley Community College
201 Constitution Hall
University of Alaska, Fairbanks 99701
Northwest Community College
P.O. Box 400, Nome 99762
Chukchi Community College
P.O. Box 297, Kotzebue 99752

MISCELLAENOUS FACTS

State capital: Juneau

Area of Alaska: 586,412 square miles or 375,296,000 acres—largest state in the union; one-fifth the size of the Lower 48.

Diameter of Alaska: East to west, 2,400 miles; north to south, 1,420 miles.

Coastline: 6,640 miles, point to point; as measured on the most detailed maps available, including islands Alaska has 33,904 miles of shoreline. Estimated tidal shoreline, including islands, inlets and shoreline to head of tidewater is 47,300 miles.

Adjacent salt water: North Pacific Ocean, Bering Sea, Chukchi Sea, Arctic Ocean.

Alaska/Canada border: 1,538 miles long; length of boundary between the Arctic Ocean and Mount Saint Elias is approximately 650 miles.

Geographic center: 63°50' north, 152° west, about 60 miles northwest of Mount McKinley.

Northernmost point: Point Barrow, 71°23' north.

Southernmost point: Tip of Amatignak Island, Aleutian Chain, 51°13'05" north.

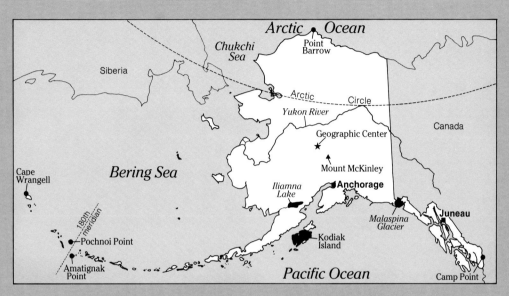

Easternmost and westernmost points: It all depends on how you look at it. According to one view, the 180th meridian—halfway around the world from the prime meridian at Greenwich, England, and the dividing line between east and west longitudes—passes through Alaska. Therefore, Alaska has both the easternmost and westernmost spots in the country! The westernmost is Amatignak Island, 179°10′ west; and the easternmost is Pochnoi Point, 179°46′ east. On the other hand, if you are facing north, east is to your right and west to your left. Therefore, the westernmost point is Cape Wrangell, Attu Island, 172°27′ east; and the easternmost is in Southeastern Alaska near Camp Point, 129°59′ west.

Farthest north supermarket: In Barrow; constructed on stilts to prevent snow buildup, at a cost of $4 million.

Tallest mountain: McKinley, 20,320 feet.

Largest natural fresh-water lake: Iliamna, 1,000 square miles.

Longest river: Yukon, 1,400 miles in Alaska; 1,875 total.

Largest glacier: Malaspina, 2,937 square miles.

Largest city in population: Anchorage, an estimated 195,000 to 197,000 in mid-1979.

State motto: "North to the Future."

State flower: Forget-me-not, by an act of the Territorial legislature April 28, 1917. The choice previously had been endorsed by the Grand Igloo of the Pioneers of Alaska.

State bird: Willow ptarmigan, declared the official bird of the territory February 4, 1955.

State tree: Sitka spruce, by an act of the 1962 State Legislature.

State fish: King salmon, by an act of the State Legislature, March 25, 1963.

State gem: Jade.

State mineral: Gold.

State sport: Dog mushing.

State flag: Big Dipper and North Star in gold on blue field.

State song: "Alaska's Flag."

Oldest building: Erskine House in Kodiak, built by the Russians, probably between 1793 and 1796.

Alaska Geographic Back Issues

The North Slope, Vol. 1, No. 1. Charter issue of *ALASKA GEOGRAPHIC*. Out of print.

One Man's Wilderness, Vol. 1, No. 2. The story of a dream shared by many, fulfilled by few: a man goes into the bush, builds a cabin and shares his incredible wilderness experience. Color photos. 116 pages, $7.95

Admiralty . . . Island in Contention, Vol. 1, No. 3. An intimate and multifaceted view of Admiralty: its geological and historical past, its present-day geography, wildlife and sparse human population. Color photos. 78 pages, $5.00

Fisheries of the North Pacific: History, Species, Gear & Processes, Vol. 1, No. 4. Out of print.

The Alaska-Yukon Wild Flowers Guide, Vol. 2, No. 1. First Northland flower book with both large, color photos and detailed drawings of every species described. Features 160 species, common and scientific names and growing height. 112 pages, $7.95

Richard Harrington's Yukon, Vol. 2, No. 2. A collection of 277 stunning color photos by Canadian photographer-writer Richard Harrington captures the Yukon in all its seasons and moods, from Watson Lake to Herschel Island. 103 pages, $7.95

Prince William Sound, Vol. 2, No. 3. Out of print.

Yakutat: The Turbulent Crescent, Vol. 2, No. 4. Out of print.

Glacier Bay: Old Ice, New Land, Vol. 3, No. 1. The expansive wilderness of Southeastern Alaska's Glacier Bay National Monument unfolds in crisp text and color photographs. Records the flora and fauna of the area, its natural history, with hike and cruise information, plus a large-scale color map. 132 pages, $9.95

The Land: Eye of the Storm, Vol. 3, No. 2. Out of print.

Richard Harrington's Antarctic, Vol. 3, No. 3. The Canadian photojournalist guides readers through remote and little understood regions of the Antarctic and Subantarctic. More than 200 color photos and a large fold-out map. 104 pages, $8.95

The Silver Years of the Alaska Canned Salmon Industry: An Album of Historical Photos, Vol. 3, No. 4. Commemorates a boom or bust era in Alaska's romantic history, and more than 293 photos record the history of the industry—late 19th century to the present. Text links the photographs by subject—canneries, boats and gear, transportation. 168 pages, $7.95

Alaska's Volcanoes: Northern Link in the Ring of Fire, Vol. 4, No. 1. Scientific overview supplemented with eyewitness accounts of Alaska's historic volcano eruptions. Includes color and black-and-white photos and a schematic description of the effects of plate movement upon volcanic activity. 88 pages, $7.95

The Brooks Range: Environmental Watershed, Vol. 4, No. 2. Looks at early exploration and at controversy over uses for the region: Native land claims, recreation, proposed national parks and development of resources. Maps, color photos. 112 pages, $9.95

Kodiak: Island of Change, Vol. 4, No. 3. Although half the size of New Jersey, and once the administrative center of Russian Alaska, the 3,588-square-mile island of Kodiak remains well off the beaten path. Past, present and future—everything from Russian exploration to the present-day quest for oil. Maps, color photos. 96 pages, $7.95

Wilderness Proposals: Which Way for Alaska's Lands?, Vol. 4, No. 4. Out of print.

Cook Inlet Country, Vol. 5, No. 1. A visual tour of the region—its communities, big and small, and its countryside. Begins at the southern tip of the Kenai Peninsula, circles Turnagain Arm and Knik Arm for a close-up view of Anchorage, and visits the Matanuska and Susitna valleys and the wild, west side of the inlet. 144 pages; 230 color photos, separate map. $9.95

Southeast: Alaska's Panhandle, Vol. 5, No. 2. Most colorful edition to date, exploring Southeastern Alaska's maze of fjords and islands, mossy forests and glacier-draped mountains—from Dixon Entrance to Icy Bay, including all of the state's fabled Inside Passage. Along the way are profiles of every town, together with a look at the region's history, economy, people, attractions and future. Includes large fold-out map and seven area maps. 192 pages, $9.95.

Bristol Bay Basin, Vol. 5, No. 3. Explores the land and the people of the region known to many as the commercial salmon-fishing capital of Alaska. Illustrated with contemporary color and historic black-and-white photos. Includes a large fold-out map of the region. 96 pages, $9.95.

Alaska Whales and Whaling, Vol. 5, No. 4. The wonders of whales in Alaska—their life cycles, travels and travails—are examined, with an authoritative history of commercial and subsistence whaling in the North. Includes a fold-out poster of 14 major whale species in Alaska in perspective, color photos and illustrations, with historical photos and line drawings. 144 pages, $9.95.

Yukon-Kuskokwim Delta, Vol. 6, No. 1. Dozens of fascinating Eskimo villages dot the sprawling landscape of the Delta, a true "last frontier" seeking a balance between rapid change and the maintenance of old ways. Included are more than 100 color photographs and a large fold-out map of the region, which extends north along the Bering Sea coast from Cape Newenham to Stebbins, and inland to a point where the Delta Eskimo villages blend with the Interior Athabascan culture. Includes large-scale fold-out map. 96 pages, $9.95.

Aurora Borealis: The Amazing Northern Lights, Vol. 6, No. 2. The northern lights—in ancient times seen as a dreadful forecast of doom, in modern days an inspiration to countless poets. Here one of the world's leading experts—Dr. S.-I. Akasofu of the University of Alaska—explains in an easily understood manner, aided by many diagrams and spectacular color and black-and-white photos, what causes the aurora, how it works, how and why scientists are studying it today and its implications for our future. 96 pages, $7.95.

Alaska's Native People, Vol. 6, No. 3. In the largest edition to date—result of several years of research—the editors examine the varied worlds of the Inupiat Eskimo, Yup'ik Eskimo, Athabascan, Aleut, Tlingit, Haida and Tsimshian. Most photos are by Lael Morgan, *ALASKA*° magazine's roving editor, who since 1974 has been gathering impressions and images from virtually every Native village in Alaska. Included are sensitive, informative articles by Native writers, plus a large, four-color map detailing the Native villages and defining the language areas. 304 pages, $19.95.

The Stikine, Vol. 6, No. 4. River route to three Canadian gold strikes in the 1800's, the Stikine is the largest and most navigable of several rivers that flow from northwestern Canada through Southeastern Alaska on their way to the sea. This edition explores 400 miles of Stikine wilderness, recounts the river's paddlewheeler past and looks into the future, wondering if the Stikine will survive as one of the North's great free-flowing rivers. Illustrated with contemporary color photos and historic black-and-white; includes a large fold-out map. 96 pages, $9.95.

Alaska's Great Interior, Vol. 7, No. 1. Alaska's rich Interior country, west from the Alaska-Yukon Territory border and including the huge drainage between the Alaska Range and the Brooks Range, is covered thoroughly. Included are the region's people, communities, history, economy, wilderness areas and wildlife. Illustrated with contemporary color and historic black-and-white photos. Includes a large fold-out map. 128 pages, $9.95.

COMING ATTRACTION:

The Aleutians, Vol. 7, No 3. The fog-shrouded Aleutians are many things — home of the Aleut, a tremendous wildlife spectacle, a major World War II battleground and now the heart of a thriving new commercial fishing industry. Roving editor Lael Morgan contributes most of the text; also included are contemporary color and black-and-white photographs, and a large fold-out map. To be distributed to members in August, 1980. Price to be announced.

Green hills and blue inlets surround the communities of Unalaska and Dutch Harbor. (Lorie Kirker)

Your $20 membership in The Alaska Geographic Society includes 4 subsequent issues of *ALASKA GEOGRAPHIC*°, the Society's official quarterly. Please add $4 for non-U.S. membership.

Additional membership information available upon request. Single copies of the *ALASKA GEOGRAPHIC*° back issues are also available. When ordering, please add $1 postage/handling per copy. To order back issues send your check or money order and volumes desired to:

The Alaska Geographic Society

Box 4-EEE, Anchorage, AK 99509